Maitreya's *Distinguishing Phenomena and Pure Being*

MAITREYA'S
Distinguishing Phenomena and Pure Being
WITH COMMENTARY BY MIPHAM

DISTINGUISHING PHENOMENA AND PURE BEING
by Maitreya • The Root Text

DISTINGUISHING WISDOM AND APPEARANCE
by Mipham Jamyang Namgyal (1846-1912) • The Commentary

Translated by Jim Scott under the guidance of
Khenpo Tsültrim Gyamtso Rinpoche

SNOW LION
BOULDER

Snow Lion
An imprint of Shambhala Publications, Inc.
4720 Walnut Street
Boulder, Colorado 80301
www.shambhala.com

Drawing of Maitreya by R.D. Salga.

Printed in the United States of America

♾This edition is printed on acid-free paper that meets the
American National Standards Institute Z39.48 Standard.
♻Shambhala Publications makes every effort to print on recycled paper.
For more information please visit www.shambhala.com.
Distributed in the United States by Penguin Random House LLC
and in Canada by Random House of Canada Ltd

Text designed and typeset by Gopa & Ted2, Inc.

The Library of Congress Cataloguing-in-Publication Data
Maitreyanātha. Dharmadharmatāvibhaṅga. English & Tibetan
Maitreya's Distinguishing phenomena and pure being / with commentary by Mipham; translated by Jim Scott under the guidance of Khenpo Tsültrim Gyamtso Rinpoche. Ithaca, N.Y.: Snow Lion Publications, c2004.
216 p.: ill.; 23 cm.
ISBN 9781559392150 (pbk.: alk. paper)
BQ3080.D5322 E57 2004

Dedicated to enlightened activity in limitless forms

and to all who master or aspire to it

༄། །འཁོར་ལོ་གསུམ་པ་སྙིང་པོའི་མདོ་རྣམས་ཀྱི། །དགོངས་དོན་མ་ནོར་ཇི་བཞིན་
རྟོགས་པ་ལ། །རྒྱུད་བླ་དང་ནི་ཆོས་ཉིད་རྣམ་འབྱེད་ལ། །ཐོས་བསམ་སྒོམ་གསུམ་བྱེད་
པ་གལ་ཆེན་ཡིན། །གནས་ལུགས་བདེ་སྟོང་ཕྱག་རྒྱ་ཆེན་པོ་དང་། །རིག་སྟོང་རྫོགས་
པ་ཆེན་པོ་རྟོགས་པ་ལའང་། །གཞུང་མཆོག་གཉིས་ཀྱི་དགོངས་དོན་རྟོགས་པ་འདི།
།ཆེན་པོ་གཉིས་ལ་ཤིན་ཏུ་གལ་ཆེན་ཡིན།
ཞེས་གསུངས་སོ།

In the Third Turning of the Wheel of Dharma,
The Buddha taught on the Buddha Nature.
In order to unerringly realize the Buddha Nature, just as it is,
It is important to study, reflect, and meditate on
The Treatise on Buddha Nature and *Distinguishing Phenomena and Pure Being*.

In order to realize abiding reality, Mahamudra, bliss-emptiness,
And Dzogchen, awareness-emptiness,
Realizing the meaning of these two supreme texts is very important.

—Khenpo Tsültrim Gyamtso Rinpoche

Contents

Translator's Preface 11
The Root Text 15
The Commentary 55
The Author's Introduction 57
The explication of the treatise 67

I. The meaning of the title 67

II. The translators' homage 67

III. The main body of the text 69
A The verse introducing the author's intention 69
B The actual body of the treatise 71
1 The brief presentation 71
I) The points comprising the essential subject matter 71
II) The defining traits of each of these 75
A) *The definition of phenomena* 75
B) *The definition of pure being* 77
III) The rationale underlying these traits 79
IV) Examining both for sameness and difference 83
2 The expanded explanation 85
I) The expanded explanation of phenomena 85
A) A presentation of the headings 85

B) An explanation of each of these 87
(1) A passing reference to the first three points. 87
(2) An explanation of the last three points. 89
(I) The explanation of the two types of ground. 89
(A) A brief presentation of both in common 89
(B) An expanded explanation of the meaning of each. 91
1) Experience comprising a common ground. 91
2) Experience not shared in common 95
(II) How to approach reality, which is free of perceived and perceiver 97
(A) The tenet stating that there is no outer referent, only image-awareness 97
1) The lack of a perceived object discrete from the perceiver 97
2) The elimination of any further uncertainty. 101
(B) The resultant procedure for approaching reality, the freedom from perceived and perceiver 107
II) The expanded explanation of pure being 113
A) A brief presentation of the headings. 113
B) The expanded explanation of these six 115
(1) The defining characteristics. 115
(2) The ground. 115
(3) Definitive verification 117
(4) Encounter 117
(5) Recollection 119
(6) Complete immersion into its core. 121
(I) The character of ultimate transformation 121
(II) The expanded explanation of its distinctive features 123

(A) The brief presentation of the headings . . . 123
(B) The expansion on these ten . . . 125
1) The essence . . . 125
2) The ingredients . . . 127
3) The individuals . . . 131
4) The special traits . . . 133
5) The requirements . . . 135
6) The ground . . . 137
a) The brief presentation . . . 137
b) The expansion on these six points . . . 141
i) The focal requirement . . . 141
ii) Surrendering attributes . . . 143
iii) How to apply the mind correctly in practice . . . 147
iv) The defining characteristics of wisdom in terms of its effects—the sphere of experience it opens . . . 149
v) The benefits . . . 159
vi) The introduction to full understanding . . . 161
(a) The brief presentation . . . 161
(b) The expansion on that . . . 163
(i) Fully understanding the remedy . . . 163
(ii) Fully understanding the concrete characteristic . . . 165
(iii) Fully understanding the distinctive marks . . . 171
(iv) Fully understanding the five effects . . . 173
7) Mental cultivation . . . 175
8) Application . . . 185

9) The disadvantages . . . 189
10) The benefits . . . 199
3 The concluding summary employing examples to illustrate the point . . . 201

IV. The concluding statement . . . 203
The Author's Colophon . . . 205
Dedication . . . 207

Bibliography . . . 209
Notes . . . 211

Translator's Preface

In response to the express wishes of His Holiness the 16th Gyalwa Karmapa, Khenpo Tsültrim Gyamtso Rinpoche, one of the most learned and accomplished contemporary masters of the Kagyu lineage, founded The Kagyu Institute of Mahayana Studies in 1978. Its purpose was to provide formal education for Westerners in the classical texts fundamental to the lineage. In another of its aspects, this institute has provided training in the Tibetan language for those wishing to translate the texts studied. In 1987, Rinpoche renamed it Marpa Institute for Translators.

This present translation is a result of that training and is thus a product of Rinpoche's unlimited kindness towards beings, knowledge of the Dharma, and skill in transmitting it. Specifically, this translation is based on Rinpoche's word-by-word commentary, first given in Boudhanath, Kathmandu, Nepal, during the Marpa Institute's 1988 winter course and further explained either in part or in full in Singapore in 1989, at Kagyu Samye Ling in Scotland during the spring of 1990, and at Karma Triyana Dharmachakra in Woodstock, New York during June of 1991.

Distinguishing Phenomena and Pure Being was composed by Maitreya, the regent of the Lord Buddha, during the golden age of Buddhism in India. The name Maitreya means "loving kindness," a name he will continue to bear when he manifests as the fifth of the one thousand historical buddhas of our world system.

The text was recorded in written form by the noble Asanga, one of the greatest meditation masters of the two and a half millennia since Buddha Shakyamuni turned the Wheel of Dharma.

The commentary, *Distinguishing Wisdom and Appearance*, was composed by Mipham Jamyang Namgyal (1846-1912), a great master of the Nyingma lineage of Tibetan Buddhism and one of the leading figures of the Ri-me (nonsectarian) movement that began in Tibet during the middle of the nineteenth century.

The intention in publishing this translation is to provide a working basis for anyone interested in deepening their understanding of the Buddha's teachings and all those wishing to comprehend the nature of their own mind and thereby realize their full potential as sentient beings.

On Rinpoche's recommendation, this has been formatted with the Tibetan and corresponding English on facing pages as a convenient device for Tibetans wishing to study it in English and English-speakers wishing to study it in Tibetan.

In setting up the table of contents, we have followed the Tibetan outline. This style of outline was not found in the textual tradition in India but was introduced by Tibetan pandits as a means of clarifying the subject matter. That system has been adopted here with a few minor alterations instead of chapter divisions, which do not provide a particularly detailed layout.

The words of Maitreya's root text appear directly in Mipham Rinpoche's commentary. This is a style prevalent throughout the tradition, right from its infancy in India. Throughout this translation, the words of the root text are rendered in italics when they appear in the commentary. This has been done to make them easy to identify.

In this tradition, the commentary is an expansion on the root, filling in points understood between the words of the root text. First, the commentary clarifies the root; and then the root can serve its original purpose: to summarize the main points of a teaching in a brief, easy-to-remember format.

That also explains why the root texts were written in meter—to facilitate memorization. This, in turn, has served two purposes throughout the course of the tradition: to facilitate recitation of the words and to help the practitioner integrate their meaning. This way of proceeding stresses the living quality of the teaching. It is meant to be spoken and speaking it furthers its integration into one's mindstream. That is why memorization and recitation are just as relevant for contemporary practitioners as they have been for every generation of practitioners going right back to the Buddha's own students.

And that is why this root text has been translated in meter. Iambic pentameter, or classical blank verse, has been chosen here, since it fits so naturally with the cadence of the English language.

Some consideration has been paid to expressing this in idiomatic English, to illustrate the perennial relevance of these teachings. But care has also been taken to allow the respective authors to speak, using their own style of teaching, which is characterized by the ease and elegance with which they are able to organize complex statements, incredibly rich in intricate detail, to communicate utter simplicity, which is beyond all expression.

Although a lengthy introduction to the subject matter does not seem necessary, the reader may find Rinpoche's brief explanation of it helpful. It includes two points:

1) The section of the text treating of phenomena follows the Chittamatra (mind only) tradition and serves the important purpose of explaining how the mind confuses itself and thus wanders in samsara by assuming that outer perceived objects and the inner perceiving mind actually exist as two different things, just because they appear to do so.

2) The section on pure being follows the shentong Madhyamaka (empty-of-other middle way) tradition by describing the nature of mind in an affirmative fashion, as self-present wisdom-awareness, the clear light. This non-dual awareness free of all conceptual fabrications is arrived at by means of a complete transformation of ordinary dualistic consciousness. This transformation and how to accomplish it are presented here with wonderful precision and in great detail.

To anyone brave enough to read this, a word of warning. Because it belongs to the category of texts devoted to what is called "the profound aspect of the teachings," it is said to be difficult to understand and difficult to realize. So don't expect it to be easy. And, because pure being, the very content of the profound secret hidden in this text, is not a conceptual construct, don't expect it to be difficult.

In conclusion, I would like to express my deep-felt gratitude to Gerald Peters, without whose sponsorship my initial years of study with Rinpoche would not have been possible. I would also like to say a special word of heart-felt thanks to my wife, Birgit Scott, a long-time student of Rinpoche and herself a translator, who has edited this text and set up the basic format according to Rinpoche's wishes. She has checked every word against the Tibetan and brought her lucid understanding to bear on every aspect of this translation.

That this publication of the words of the coming Buddha, Maitreya, interpreting the words of the present Buddha, Shakyamuni, is a result of the wishes of the 16th Karmapa appearing during the lifetime of the 17th, Urgyen Trinle Dorje, bears witness to the living continuity of the teaching of the victors in our world.

May their teachings flourish and lead to the transformation of consciousness into wisdom for all beings and, first and foremost, for everyone listening.

Jim Scott
Aarhus, Denmark
December, 2003

DISTINGUISHING PHENOMENA AND PURE BEING

BY MAITREYA

The Root Text

༄༅། རྒྱ་གར་སྐད་དུ། དྷརྨ་དྷརྨ་ཏཱ་བི་བྷཾ་ག་ཀཱ་རི་ཀཱ།
བོད་སྐད་དུ། ཆོས་དང་ཆོས་ཉིད་རྣམ་པར་འབྱེད་པའི་ཚིག་ལེའུར་བྱས་པ།

མགོན་པོ་བྱམས་པ་ལ་ཕྱག་འཚལ་ལོ།

ཤེས་ནས་གང་ཞིག་ཡོངས་སུ་སྤང་བྱ་ཞིང་།
གཞན་འགའ་ཞིག་ནི་མངོན་སུམ་ཉིད་དུ་བྱ།
དེས་ན་དེ་དག་མཚན་ཉིད་རྣམ་དབྱེ་བ།
བྱེད་པར་འདོད་ནས་བསྟན་བཅོས་འདི་བརྩམས་སོ།

འདི་དག་ཐམས་ཅད་མདོར་བསྡུ་ན།
རྣམ་པ་གཉིས་སུ་ཤེས་བྱ་སྟེ།
ཆོས་དང་དེ་བཞིན་ཆོས་ཉིད་ཀྱིས།
ཐམས་ཅད་བསྡུས་པ་ཉིད་ཕྱིར་རོ།
དེ་ལ་ཆོས་ཀྱིས་ཕྱེ་བ་ནི།
འཁོར་བ་ཡིན་ཏེ་ཆོས་ཉིད་ཀྱིས།
རབ་ཏུ་ཕྱེ་བ་ཐེག་གསུམ་གྱི།
མྱ་ངན་ལས་ནི་འདས་པའོ།

In Sanskrit: dharmadharmatavibhagakarika

In Tibetan: chos dang chos nyid rnam par 'byed pa'i tshig le'ur byas pa

To the guardian Maitreya we bow in supplication.

Something there is to be given up fully through knowing
And something else which can only be actualized,
Because of which this treatise has been composed
With the wish to distinguish the traits defining these.

A summary of everything in brief
Should be known to include the following two motifs,
Since everything can be summarized fully in terms
Of phenomena together with pure being.
That which is classified here as phenomena
Is samsara; that which is classified precisely
As pure being is nirvana, transcendence of grief,
As this is defined by the vehicles, which are three.

དེ་ལ་ཆོས་ཀྱི་མཚན་ཉིད་ནི།
གཉིས་དང་ཇི་ལྟར་མངོན་བརྗོད་པར།
སྣང་བ་ཡང་དག་མ་ཡིན་པའི།
ཀུན་རྟོག་པ་སྟེ་མེད་སྣང་ཕྱིར།
དེས་ན་ཡང་དག་མ་ཡིན་ནོ།
དེ་ཡང་ཐམས་ཅད་དོན་མེད་ཅིང་།
རྟོག་ཙམ་ཡིན་པས་ཀུན་རྟོག་པའོ།

གཞན་ཡང་ཆོས་ཉིད་མཚན་ཉིད་ནི།
གཟུང་བ་དང་ནི་འཛིན་པ་དང་།
བརྗོད་པར་བྱ་དང་རྗོད་པར་བྱེད།
ཁྱད་མེད་དེ་བཞིན་ཉིད་ཡིན་ནོ།

མེད་པ་སྣང་ཕྱིར་འཁྲུལ་པ་ནི།
ཀུན་ནས་ཉོན་མོངས་རྒྱུ་ཡིན་ཏེ།
སྒྱུ་མའི་གླང་ཆེན་སོགས་སྣང་ཞིང་།
ཡོད་པའང་སྣང་བ་མིན་ཕྱིར་རོ།
མེད་སྣང་དག་ལས་གང་རུང་ཞིག
མེད་ན་འཁྲུལ་དང་མ་འཁྲུལ་དང་།
དེ་བཞིན་ཀུན་ནས་ཉོན་མོངས་དང་།
རྣམ་པར་བྱང་བ་མི་འཐད་དོ།

Here the traits of phenomena are defined
As duality plus assumption and formulation,
Whose appearance is the mistaken conceptual process,
Since what appears is not and is thus not real.
No referents have ever existed either
And, being but concept, consist of conceptualization.

The other factor, pure being, is defined
As suchness, in which there is no differentiation
Between a factor perceived and a perceiver,
A signifier contra a signified.

Because what does not exist appears, delusion
Provides the cause for completely afflicted states;
Since things like illusory elephants appear,
Even what does exist does not appear.
If either the lack of existence or the appearance
Were missing, delusion and freedom from delusion
And likewise states afflicted in every respect
And thorough refinement would be unjustified.

གཉིས་པོ་དག་ནི་གཅིག་ཉིད་དང་།
སོ་སོ་བ་ཡང་མ་ཡིན་ཏེ།
ཡོད་པ་དང་ནི་མེད་པ་དག
ཁྱད་པར་ཡོད་དང་མེད་ཕྱིར་རོ།

རྣམ་པ་དྲུག་གིས་ཆོས་དག་ལ།
འཇུག་པ་བླ་ན་མེད་པ་སྟེ།
མཚན་ཉིད་དང་ནི་གྲུབ་པ་དང་།
གཅིག་དང་ཐ་དད་མ་ཡིན་ཞིང་།
གནས་ནི་ཐུན་མོང་ཐུན་མོང་མིན།
གཟུང་དང་འཛིན་པར་སྣང་བ་ནི།
མེད་ལ་རབ་ཏུ་འཇུག་པས་སོ།

དེ་ལ་མཚན་ཉིད་གྲུབ་པ་དང་།
གཅིག་དང་ཐ་དད་མ་ཡིན་པ།
ཇི་ལྟར་མདོར་བསྟན་བཞིན་དུའོ།

These two are not one and the same nor do they differ,
Because, between that which exists and that which does not,
A distinction exists and yet does not exist.

Because it provides a thorough introduction
To their characteristics as well as their rationale,
Their neither being the same nor different,
The ground in common and not in common shared,
And the lack of appearance involving perceiver-perceived,
This sixpoint approach to phenomena is the best.

Of these, the defining traits and the rationale,
As well as the lack of sameness and difference,
Are just as these were demonstrated in brief.

གང་ཞིག་གང་དུ་འཁོར་བ་ན།
དེ་ནི་ཀུན་ཏུ་གནས་པ་སྟེ།
སེམས་ཅན་ཁམས་དང་སྣོད་ཀྱི་ཁམས།
སྣོད་ཀྱི་ཁམས་ནི་ཐུན་མོང་ལྟར།
རྣམ་པར་རིག་པ་ཐུན་མོང་ཡིན།
སེམས་ཅན་ཁམས་ནི་ཐུན་མོང་དང་།
ཡང་ན་ཐུན་མོང་མ་ཡིན་པའོ།

དེ་ཡང་སྐྱེ་དང་ཐ་སྙད་དང་།
རྗེས་སུ་གཟུང་དང་ཚར་གཅོད་དང་།
ཕན་པ་དང་ནི་གནོད་པ་དང་།
ཡོན་ཏན་སྐྱོན་ནི་ཕན་ཚུན་དུ།
བདག་པོ་ཉིད་ཀྱིས་ཕན་ཚུན་རྒྱུ།
ཡིན་པའི་ཕྱིར་ན་ཐུན་མོང་པའོ།

གནས་དང་རྣམ་པར་རིག་པ་དང་།
བདེ་སྡུག་ལས་དང་འཆི་འཕོ་དང་།
སྐྱེ་བ་དང་ནི་བཅིངས་བ་དང་།
གྲོལ་བ་ཐུན་མོང་མ་ཡིན་ཕྱིར།
དེ་གནས་ཐུན་མོང་མ་ཡིན་པའོ།

As long as there is someone circling somewhere,
These are the grounds in each and every case—
The constituents of beings and those of the vessel.
The constituents of the vessel appear to be shared,
The awareness being the common experience;
Some of the constituents of beings
Are experienced in common and some are not.

Further, birth and conventions, to nurture, subdue,
Benefit, harm, excellent features, and faults
Are mutually caused by way of an interchange,
Because of which these are experience shared in common.

Since the ground and awareness, happiness, suffering,
Action, transition at death, captivity, birth,
And liberation are not observed in common,
They comprise the realm of experience not shared in common.

ཕྱི་རོལ་གཟུང་བ་ཐུན་མོང་བར།
སྣང་བ་འཛིན་པའི་རྣམ་རིག་པའོ།
རྣམ་པར་ཤེས་ལས་ཕྱི་རོལ་དུ།
གྲུབ་པའི་དོན་ཡོད་མ་ཡིན་ཏེ།
ཐུན་མོང་བ་ཉིད་ཡིན་ཕྱིར་རོ།

གཅིག་ཤོས་ཐུན་མོང་མ་ཡིན་པའི།
གཟུང་བ་རྣམ་པར་རིག་པའི་དོན།
གཞན་གྱི་སེམས་ལ་སོགས་པ་ནི།
མཉམ་པར་མ་གཞག་མཉམ་གཞག་པའི།
འཛིན་པའི་རྣམ་པར་རིག་པ་ལ།
ཕན་ཚུན་ཡུལ་གྲུར་མ་ཡིན་ཏེ།
མཉམ་པར་མ་གཞག་དག་ལ་ནི།
རང་གི་རྣམ་རྟོག་སྣང་ཕྱིར་དང་།
མཉམ་པར་གཞག་པ་དག་ལ་ནི།
ཏིང་འཛིན་དེ་ཡི་སྤྱོད་ཡུལ་དེའི།
གཟུགས་བརྙན་རབ་ཏུ་སྣང་ཕྱིར་རོ།

What appear to be outer, perceivable in common,
Are perceiving awareness; they are not referents
Existing as something extrinsic to consciousness,
Precisely because they are common experiences.

The counterpart is the one in which what is perceived
Is not shared in common. Here awareness' referent
Is the minds and so on associated with others.
These do not comprise an object of mutual exchange
For perceiving awareness not resting nor resting poised,
Because, for those not resting in equipoise,
It is but their own conceptions that appear;
And because, for those who are resting in equipoise,
It is its faithful reflection that appears
As the object encountered during samadhi absorption.

གཟུང་བར་སྣང་བ་མེད་གྱུར་ན།
འཛིན་པར་སྣང་བ་མེད་གྱུར་བོ།
དེ་ལས་ཀྱང་ནི་གཟུང་བ་དང་།
འཛིན་པར་སྣང་བ་མེད་པ་ལ།
འཇུག་པ་གྲུབ་སྟེ་ཐོབ་མེད་པའི།
ཀུན་ནས་ལྡང་བ་གྲུབ་པས་སོ།
གཉིས་སུ་ཡོངས་སུ་མ་གྲུབ་པར།
རབ་ཏུ་གྲུབ་པ་ཡིན་ཕྱིར་རོ།

རྣམ་པ་དྲུག་གིས་ཆོས་ཉིད་ལ།
འཇུག་པ་བླ་ན་མེད་པ་སྟེ།
མཚན་ཉིད་ཀུན་ཏུ་གནས་པ་དང་།
ངེས་པར་འབྱེད་དང་རེག་པ་དང་།
རྗེས་སུ་དྲན་དང་དེའི་བདག་ཉིད།
ཉེ་བར་སོན་ལ་འཇུག་པས་སོ།

If what appears as perceived does not exist,
Whatever appears as perceiver does not exist;
Due to this, there is also a rationale
Behind the breakthrough to freedom from this appearance
Of perceived and perceiver, because without beginning
A volatile state prevails; and because duality's
Not existing at all is what really exists.

Through introducing traits and a ground at all times,
Definitive verification as well as encounter,
Recollection and immersion into its core,
This sixpoint approach to pure being is unsurpassed.

མཚན་ཉིད་མདོ་ནི་ཇི་ལྟ་བཞིན།

གནས་ནི་ཆོས་རྣམས་ཐམས་ཅད་དང་།
གསུང་རབ་མདོ་སྡེ་ཐམས་ཅད་དོ།

དེ་ལ་ངེས་པར་འབྱེད་པ་ནི།
ཐེག་པ་ཆེན་པོའི་མདོ་སྡེ་ལ།
བརྟེན་པའི་ཚུལ་བཞིན་ཡིད་བྱེད་པས།
བསྡུས་པའི་སྦྱོར་ལམ་ཐམས་ཅད་དོ།

རིག་པ་ཡང་དག་ལྟ་ཐོབ་ཕྱིར།
མཐོང་བའི་ལམ་གྱིས་མངོན་སུམ་གྱི།
ཚུལ་དུ་དེ་བཞིན་ཉིད་ཐོབ་ཅིང་།
ཉམས་སུ་མྱོང་བ་གང་ཡིན་པའོ།

རྗེས་སུ་དྲན་པ་རིག་པས་ནི།
མཐོང་བའི་དོན་ལ་སྒོམ་ལམ་གྱི།
བྱང་ཆུབ་ཕྱོགས་ཀྱིས་བསྡུས་པ་སྟེ།
དེ་ནི་དྲི་མ་སེལ་བའི་ཕྱིར།

The defining traits in brief are just as they are.

The ground consists of the whole of phenomena
And supreme teachings, the whole of the sutra collections.

The term "definitive verification of this"
Refers to the whole of the path of application,
Comprised of appropriate mental cultivation
Based on the sutra collections of Mahayana.

The encounter attained because of authentic view
Is the path of vision, on which the suchness attained
Is in a fashion direct, whatever experienced.

Although reality *has* been seen by awareness,
Recollection—the path of meditation,
Comprised of factors inducing enlightenment—
Is needed to eliminate the stains.

དེ་ལ་དེ་ཡི་བདག་ཉིད་དུ།
ཉེ་བར་སྟོན་པ་དེ་བཞིན་ཉིད།
དྲི་མ་མེད་པར་གྱུར་པ་ན།
ཐམས་ཅད་དེ་བཞིན་ཉིད་ཙམ་དུ།
སྣང་བ་དེ་ཡང་གནས་གྱུར་པ།
གྲུབ་པ་ཡིན་ནོ་༔

༔རྣམ་པ་བཅུས།
གནས་ཡོངས་གྱུར་ལ་འཇུག་པ་ནི།
བླ་ན་མེད་པ་ཉིད་ཡིན་ཏེ།
ངོ་བོ་རྫས་དང་གང་ཟག་དང་།
ཁྱད་པར་དགོས་པ་གནས་དང་ནི།
ཡིད་ལ་བྱེད་དང་སྦྱོར་བ་དང་།
ཉེས་དམིགས་ཕན་ཡོན་འཇུག་པས་སོ།

དེ་ལ་ངོ་བོར་འཇུག་པ་ནི།
གློ་བུར་བ་ཡི་དྲི་མ་དང་།
དེ་བཞིན་ཉིད་མི་སྣང་བ་དང་།
སྣང་བའི་དོན་དུ་དེ་བཞིན་ཉིད།
དྲི་མ་མེད་པ་གང་ཡིན་པའོ།

Here, immersion into its core complete,
Is suchness rendered free of any stain,
Where all appear exclusively as suchness—
And this completes the transformation as well.

This tenpoint presentation of transformation
Provides an unsurpassable introduction,
Because it is the way to approach the essence,
Ingredients and individuals,
The special traits, requirements, and ground,
Mental cultivation and application,
The disadvantages and benefits.

The essence of transformation is introduced
As suchness freed of stain, and what that means
Is superficial stains appear no longer
And that which manifests is now the suchness.

དངོས་པོ་རྫས་ལ་འཇུག་པ་ནི།
ཐུན་མོང་སྣོད་ཀྱི་རྣམ་རིག་པ།
དེ་བཞིན་ཉིད་དུ་གྱུར་པ་དང་།
མདོ་སྡེ་ཆོས་ཀྱི་དབྱིངས་ཉིད་ཀྱི།
དེ་བཞིན་ཉིད་དུ་གྱུར་པ་དང་།
ཐུན་མོང་མིན་པ་སེམས་ཅན་གྱི།
ཁམས་ཀྱི་རྣམ་པར་རིག་པ་ཡི།
དེ་བཞིན་ཉིད་དུ་གྱུར་པའོ།

གང་ཟག་དག་ལ་འཇུག་པ་ནི།
དང་པོ་གཉིས་ནི་སངས་རྒྱས་དང་།
བྱང་ཆུབ་སེམས་དཔའ་རྣམས་ཀྱི་ནི།
དེ་བཞིན་ཉིད་ཡོངས་གྱུར་པ་སྟེ།
ཕྱི་མ་ཉན་ཐོས་རྣམས་དང་ནི།
རང་སངས་རྒྱས་ཀྱི་ཡང་ཡིན་ནོ།

To introduce the ingredients, or contents:
Awareness in the form of the vessel shared
Undergoes a transformation to suchness;
The sutras undergo a transformation
Into the suchness, the actual dharmadhatu;
And beings' awareness-components not shared in common
Undergo a transformation to suchness.

The approach as related to individuals:
The first two of these are transformations to suchness
Pertaining to buddhas as well as to bodhisattvas;
The last of these pertains additionally
To Shravakas as well as Pratyekabuddhas.

ཁྱད་པར་ཅན་ལ་འཇུག་པ་ནི།
སངས་རྒྱས་བྱང་ཆུབ་སེམས་དཔའ་རྣམས།
ཞིང་ཡོངས་དག་པའི་ཁྱད་པར་དང་།
ཆོས་སྐུ་ལོངས་སྤྱོད་རྫོགས་པ་དང་།
སྤྲུལ་སྐུ་ཐོབ་པས་གཟིགས་པ་དང་།
འདོམས་པ་དང་ནི་དབང་འབྱོར་ཉིད།
ཐོབ་པའི་ཁྱད་པར་ལས་ཡིན་ནོ།

དགོས་པ་རྟོགས་ལ་འཇུག་པ་ནི།
སྔོན་གྱི་སྨོན་ལམ་ཁྱད་པར་དང་།
ཐེག་པ་ཆེན་པོ་སྟོན་པ་ནི།
དམིགས་པའི་ཁྱད་པར་ས་བཅུ་ལ།
རབ་ཏུ་སྦྱོར་བའི་ཁྱད་པར་རོ།

གནས་སམ་རྟེན་ལ་འཇུག་པ་ནི།
རྣམ་པར་མི་རྟོག་ཡེ་ཤེས་ལ།
འཇུག་པ་རྣམ་པ་དྲུག་གིས་ཏེ།
དམིགས་དང་མཚན་མ་སྤངས་པ་དང་།
ཡང་དག་པ་ཡི་སྦྱོར་བ་དང་།
མཚན་ཉིད་དང་ནི་ཕན་ཡོན་དང་།
ཡོངས་སུ་ཤེས་ལ་འཇུག་པས་སོ།

The introduction to traits especially advanced
Pertains to buddhas as well as to bodhisattvas:
The distinguishing trait of totally pure domains;
That which is gained through attaining the dharmakaya;
Sambhogakaya; as well as nirmanakaya—
The insight, instruction, and consummate mastery—
Are attainments distinctively greater comparatively.

The introduction to realizing what is required:
The distinguishing factor of previous wishing prayers;
The distinguishing factor of Mahayana teaching
As focal point; and the further distinguishing factor
Of effective application to all ten levels.

The introduction involving the ground or support
Is into original nonconceptual wisdom
As this is approached in a manner involving six points,
Since the focal requirement, attributes surrendered,
The correct way to apply the mind in practice,
The defining characteristics and benefits,
And full understanding are hereby introduced.

དེ་ལ་དང་པོ་དམིགས་པ་ལ།
འཇུག་པ་རྣམ་པ་བཞིར་ཤེས་བྱ།
ཐེག་པ་ཆེན་པོ་སྟོན་པ་དང་།
དེ་ལ་མོས་དང་ངེས་པ་དང་།
ཚོགས་ནི་ཡོངས་སུ་རྫོགས་པས་སོ།

གཉིས་པ་མཚན་མ་སྤངས་པ་ལ།
འཇུག་པ་ཡང་ནི་རྣམ་བཞི་སྟེ།
མི་མཐུན་པ་དང་གཉེན་པོ་དང་།
དེ་བཞིན་ཉིད་དང་རྟོགས་པ་ཡི།
མཚན་མ་དག་ནི་སྤངས་པས་སོ།
འདིས་ནི་རིམ་པ་ཇི་ལྟ་བཞིན།
རགས་དང་འབྲིང་དང་ཕྲ་མོ་དང་།
རིང་དུ་རྗེས་སུ་འབྲེལ་བ་ཡི།
མཚན་མ་ཡོངས་སུ་སྤངས་པ་ཡིན།

The first of these, the focal requirement,
Should be known to be introduced in four points,
Since what is required is Mahayana teachings,
Commitment to these, along with certitude
And fully completing the two accumulations.

The second, which treats of surrendering attributes,
Is also introduced by way of four points,
Since what is unfavorable and the remedies,
The suchness as well as the realization of this
Are attributes whose surrender leads the way.
By doing this in respective order as follows—
The coarse and the middling followed by those which are fine,
And those which persist for a very long time indeed—
These attributes are surrendered entirely.

ཡང་དག་པ་ཡི་སྦྱོར་བ་ལ།
འཇུག་པ་ཡང་ནི་རྣམ་བཞི་སྟེ།
དམིགས་པ་ཡི་ནི་སྦྱོར་བ་དང་།
མི་དམིགས་པ་ཡི་སྦྱོར་བ་དང་།
དམིགས་པ་མི་དམིགས་སྦྱོར་བ་དང་།
མི་དམིགས་དམིགས་པའི་སྦྱོར་བའོ།

དེ་ལ་མཚན་ཉིད་འཇུག་པ་ནི།
རྣམ་པ་གསུམ་གྱིས་ཤེས་བྱ་སྟེ།

ཆོས་ཉིད་གནས་པ་ཉིད་ལས་ནི།
གཉིས་སུ་མེད་ཅིང་བརྗོད་མེད་པའི།
ཆོས་ཉིད་རབ་ཏུ་གནས་ཕྱིར་རོ།

The introduction to practicing wisdom correctly
Entails the following four specific aspects:
Practice involving something to focus on;
Practice involving nothing to focus on;
Practice involving no subject to focus on;
Practice whose focus is nothing to focus on.

The defining characteristics here encountered
Should be known to consist of the following three aspects,
Since one effect is repose in pure being,
Which means to actually live in pure being,
The non-dualistic and inexpressible;

སྣང་བ་མེད་ལས་གཉིས་དང་ནི།
ཇི་ལྟར་མངོན་པར་བརྗོད་པ་དང་།
དབང་པོ་ཡུལ་དང་རྣམ་རིག་དང་།
སྣོད་ཀྱི་འཇིག་རྟེན་སྣང་མེད་ཕྱིར།
དེས་ན་འདིས་ནི་བརྟག་མེད་པ།
བསྟན་དུ་མེད་པ་གནས་མེད་པ།
སྣང་བ་མེད་ཅིང་རྣམ་རིག་མེད།
གནས་མེད་པ་ཞེས་བྱ་བ་སྟེ།
རྣམ་པར་མི་རྟོག་ཡེ་ཤེས་ཀྱི།
མཚན་ཉིད་མདོ་བཞིན་བརྗོད་པ་ཡིན།

སྣང་བ་ལས་ནི་ཆོས་ཐམས་ཅད།
ནམ་མཁའི་དཀྱིལ་མཉམ་སྣང་ཕྱིར་རོ།
འདུ་བྱེད་ཐམས་ཅད་སྒྱུ་མ་སོགས།
ལྟ་བུར་སྣང་བ་ཡིན་ཕྱིར་རོ།

ཕན་ཡོན་འཇུག་པ་རྣམ་བཞི་སྟེ།
ཆོས་སྐུ་རྫོགས་པར་ཐོབ་པ་དང་།
གོང་ན་མེད་པའི་བདེ་ཐོབ་དང་།
གཟིགས་པ་དབང་འབྱོར་ཐོབ་པ་དང་།
སྟོན་ལ་དབང་འབྱོར་ཐོབ་པའོ།

And one effect relates to appearances' absence,
Where duality, assumption and formulation,
Faculties, objects, principles of awareness,
And vessel-like worlds' appearances are absent;
So these correspond to there being no observation,
No description, no ground and no appearances,
No principles of awareness, and no place,
Which is how the sutras express the traits
Defining original nonconceptual wisdom;
And one effect relates to appearances' presence,
Since experience of every phenomenon
Is equivalent to the center of open space,
And formations all are appearances like illusions.

The four points introducing the benefits
Include the complete attainment of dharmakaya,
Attainment of bliss which nothing can exceed,
Attainment of mastery over the power of insight,
And attainment of mastery over the power to teach.

ཡོངས་སུ་ཤེས་ལ་འཇུག་པ་ནི།
རྣམ་པ་བཞི་རུ་ཤེས་བྱ་སྟེ།
གཉེན་པོ་ཡོངས་སུ་ཤེས་པ་དང་།
མཚན་ཉིད་ཡོངས་སུ་ཤེས་པ་དང་།
ཁྱད་པར་ཡོངས་སུ་ཤེས་པ་དང་།
ལས་ལྔ་ཡོངས་སུ་ཤེས་པའོ།

དེ་ལ་གཉེན་པོ་ཤེས་པ་ནི།
རྣམ་པར་མི་རྟོག་ཡེ་ཤེས་ཏེ།
ཆོས་དང་གང་ཟག་འཛིན་པ་དང་།
ཡོངས་གྱུར་པ་དང་ཐ་དད་དང་།
སྐྱུར་བ་འདེབས་པ་ཉིད་ཡིན་ཏེ།
མེད་པ་འཛིན་པ་རྣམ་པ་ལྔའི།
གཉེན་པོ་བསྟན་པ་ཡིན་ཕྱིར་རོ།

མཚན་ཉིད་ཡོངས་སུ་ཤེས་པ་ནི།
ཡིད་ལ་མི་བྱེད་ཡང་དག་འདས།
ཉེ་བར་ཞི་དང་ངོ་བོའི་དོན།
མངོན་རྟགས་འཛིན་པ་རྣམ་པ་ལྔ།
སྤྱངས་པའི་རང་གི་མཚན་ཉིད་དོ།

The introduction to thorough understanding
Should be known to include the following four points:
A full understanding regarding the remedy;
A full understanding regarding the characteristic;
A full understanding regarding distinctive marks;
And a full understanding regarding the five effects.

What is to be understood as the remedy here
Is nonconceptualizing original wisdom,
Since perceiving phenomena, individuals,
An alteration as well as dichotomy,
Denial as well, when this is entertained,
Are five distinct forms of perception of non-existents
For which it is taught to comprise the remedy.

Full understanding regarding the characteristic:
A lack of the process of thought and correct transcendence,
Tranquilization, things in their composition,
And predetermination are the five
The exclusion of which is the concrete characteristic.

ཁྱད་པར་ཡོངས་སུ་ཤེས་པ་ནི།
རྣམ་པར་མི་རྟོག་པ་ཉིད་དང་།
ཉི་ཚེ་བ་ནི་མ་ཡིན་དང་།
གནས་མེད་པ་དང་གཏན་དུ་དང་།
གོང་ན་མེད་པའི་རྣམ་པ་སྟེ།
ཁྱད་པར་རྣམ་པ་ལྔ་ཡིན་ནོ།

ཐ་མ་ལས་ཡོངས་ཤེས་པ་ནི།
རྣམ་རྟོག་རིང་དུ་བྱེད་པ་དང་།
བླ་ན་མེད་པའི་བདེ་སྐྱེར་དང་།
ཉོན་མོངས་པ་དང་ཤེས་བྱ་ཡི།
སྒྲིབ་པ་ཐུལ་བར་བྱེད་པ་སྟེ།
དེ་ཡི་རྗེས་ལས་ཐོབ་པ་ཡི།
ཡེ་ཤེས་ཤེས་བྱའི་རྣམ་པ་ནི།
ཐམས་ཅད་ལ་ནི་འཇུག་པ་དང་།
སངས་རྒྱས་ཞིང་ནི་སྦྱོང་བ་དང་།
སེམས་ཅན་ཡོངས་སུ་སྨིན་བྱེད་དང་།
རྣམ་པ་ཐམས་ཅད་མཁྱེན་པ་ཉིད།
གཏོད་ཅིང་སྐྱེར་བར་བྱེད་པ་སྟེ།
རྣམ་ལྔ་ལས་ཀྱི་ཁྱད་པར་རོ།

Completely understanding its marks refers
To its being free of conceptualization as such,
To the fact that it is not transitional,
To its not remaining while being there all along,
And its hallmark of being completely unexcelled;
These make up its five distinctive marks.

The last, the full understanding of its effects,
Includes its lasting effect on conceptualization;
Its affording unsurpassable happiness;
Its effecting elimination of obscurations—
Afflicted emotions and cognitive obscurations;
The original wisdom attained in the wake of this
Provides the access to every aspect of knowledge;
It enables achieving attunement with buddha-fields
And thorough maturation of sentient beings,
And brings about revelation and transmission
Of knowledge which is complete in every aspect;
These five are the special features of the effects.

ཡིད་ལ་བྱེད་ལ་འཇུག་པ་ནི།

རྣམ་པར་མི་རྟོག་ཡེ་ཤེས་ལ།

འཇུག་པར་འདོད་པའི་གང་ཟག་ནི།

བྱང་ཆུབ་སེམས་དཔའ་གང་ཡིན་པ།

འདི་ལྟར་ཡིད་ལ་བྱེད་པ་སྟེ།

དེ་བཞིན་ཉིད་ནི་མི་ཤེས་པས།

མི་བདེན་པར་ནི་ཡོངས་བརྟགས་པའི།

ས་བོན་ཐམས་ཅད་པ་ཞེས་པ།

མེད་པ་གཉིས་སུ་སྣང་བའི་རྒྱུ།

དེ་ལ་བརྟེན་པའི་ཐ་དད་རྒྱུ།

དེས་ནི་རྒྱུ་དང་འབྲས་བུར་བཅས།

སྣང་དུ་ཟིན་ཀྱང་མེད་པའོ།

དེ་སྣང་ཆོས་ཉིད་མི་སྣང་ཞིང་།

དེ་མི་སྣང་བས་ཆོས་ཉིད་སྣང་།

དེ་ལྟར་ཚུལ་བཞིན་ཡིད་བྱེད་ན།

བྱང་ཆུབ་སེམས་དཔའི་མི་རྟོག་པའི།

ཡེ་ཤེས་ལ་ནི་འཇུག་པའོ།

The introduction to mental cultivation:
For individuals wishing to cross the threshold
Into original nonconceptual wisdom,
For any bodhisattva, Awakening Hero,
Here is how to cultivate the mind.
By virtue of one's ignorance of suchness
The "store of all seeds" of what is unreal, mere invention,
Is the cause for two which do not exist to appear;
And, with that as the base, there are grounds for diversification,
Due to which the cause and effects as well,
In spite of appearing, still do not exist.
With that appearing, pure being does not appear;
Through that not appearing, pure being indeed appears.
Through such cultivation of mind, when properly done,
The Bodhisattva steps across the brink
Into original nonconceptual wisdom.

དེ་ལྟར་དམིགས་ལས་རྣམ་རིག་ཙམ།
དམིགས་ལས་དོན་རྣམས་མི་དམིགས་དང་།
དོན་རྣམས་མི་དམིགས་པ་ལས་ནི།
རྣམ་པར་རིག་ཙམ་མི་དམིགས་དང་།
དེ་མི་དམིགས་ལས་གཉིས་པོ་ནི།
ཁྱད་པར་མེད་པའི་དམིགས་ལ་འཇུག
དེ་གཉིས་ཁྱད་པར་མི་དམིགས་པ།
དེ་ནི་རྣམ་པར་མི་རྟོག་པའི།
ཡེ་ཤེས་ཡུལ་མེད་དམིགས་མེད་པ།
མཚན་མ་ཐམས་ཅད་མི་དམིགས་པས།
རབ་ཕྱེ་བ་ནི་ཡིན་ཕྱིར་རོ།

སྦྱོར་བས་ས་ལ་འཇུག་པ་ནི།
རྣམ་པ་བཞི་རུ་ཤེས་བྱ་སྟེ།
མོས་པས་རབ་ཏུ་སྦྱོར་བས་ནི།
མོས་པས་སྤྱོད་པའི་ས་ལ་སྟེ།
ངེས་པར་འབྱེད་པའི་གནས་སྐབས་སོ།
སོ་སོར་རབ་ཏུ་རྟོགས་པ་ཡི།
སྦྱོར་བས་ས་ནི་དང་པོ་སྟེ།
དེ་ཉིད་རིག་པའི་གནས་སྐབས་སོ།

Through focusing thus, mere awareness is focused on,
Through which there are no referents to focus on;
Through there being no referents that could be focused on,
There is no such mere awareness to focus on;
Through that not existing on which to focus, the verge
Is crossed into focusing free of this twofold division;
No split into two existing on which to focus,
This is original nonconceptual wisdom,
Since this is what is defined with the utmost precision
As that which involves no object, no focusing,
No attributes on which to focus at all.

The penetration of levels through application
Should be known to entail the following four steps:
Through intense application involving informed commitment,
The stage where training is done through informed commitment
Comprises the step of definitive verification.
To connect with superior, firsthand realization
Is the first of the levels, the stage the precise is encountered.

བསྒོམ་པས་རབ་ཏུ་སྦྱོར་བས་ནི།
མ་དག་པ་ཡི་ས་དག་དང་།
དག་པའི་ས་ནི་གསུམ་པོ་སྟེ།
དེ་ནི་རྗེས་དྲན་གནས་སྐབས་སོ།
མཐར་ཕྱིན་པ་ལ་སྦྱོར་བས་ནི།
ལྷུན་གྱིས་གྲུབ་པར་སངས་རྒྱས་ཀྱི།
མཛད་པ་རྒྱུན་མི་འཆད་ཕྱིར་ཏེ།
དེ་ནི་དེ་ཡི་བདག་ཉིད་དུ།
ཉེ་བར་འགྲོ་བའི་གནས་སྐབས་སོ།

ཉེས་དམིགས་དག་ལ་འཇུག་པ་ནི།
གནས་ཡོངས་གྱུར་པ་མེད་པ་ཡི།
ཉེས་དམིགས་བཞི་སྟེ་ཉོན་མོངས་པ།
མི་འཇུག་རྟེན་མེད་ཉེས་པ་དང་།
ལམ་འཇུག་རྟེན་མེད་ཉེས་པ་དང་།
མྱ་ངན་འདས་པའི་གང་ཟག་རྣམས།
གདགས་པའི་གཞི་མེད་ཉེས་པ་དང་།
བྱང་ཆུབ་གསུམ་གྱི་ཁྱད་པར་དག
གདགས་པའི་གཞི་མེད་ཉེས་པའོ།

Through intense application employing meditation,
The impure levels followed by those which are pure
Are what comprise the stage of recollection.
Through application involving final perfection,
The spontaneous deeds of a buddha continually flow;
Hence this is the stage of immersion into the core.

The introduction to disadvantages
Includes the four which would follow as a result
Of there being no transformation; namely, the flaw
That preventing afflictions' entry would lack a support;
The flaw of the path's introduction lacking support;
The flaw of there being no basis of imputation
For speaking of individuals reaching nirvana;
As well as the flaw of no basis of imputation
For distinctions between three forms of enlightenment.

བཟློག་ནས་ཕན་ཡོན་འཇུག་པ་ནི།
རྣམ་པ་བཞི་རུ་ཤེས་པར་བྱའོ།

མེད་པའི་ཆོས་རྣམས་སྣང་བའི་དཔེ།
སྒྱུ་མ་རྨི་ལམ་སོགས་པ་བཞིན།
གནས་ཡོངས་གྱུར་པ་དཔེར་བྱ་ན།
ནམ་མཁའ་གསེར་དང་ཆུ་སོགས་བཞིན།

ཆོས་དང་ཆོས་ཉིད་རྣམ་པར་འབྱེད་པའི་ཚིག་ལེའུར་བྱས་པ།
མགོན་པོ་བྱམས་པས་མཛད་པ་རྫོགས་སོ། །

ཁ་ཆེའི་མཁན་པོ་མ་ཧཱ་ཛ་ན་དང༌། ལོ་ཙཱ་བ་དགེ་སློང་སེང་གེ་རྒྱལ་མཚན་
གྱིས་བསྒྱུར་ཅིང་ཞུས་ཏེ་གཏན་ལ་ཕབ་པའོ། །

The introduction to the benefits
Should be known to include these four, but in the reverse.

To show how phenomena not existing appear,
They are likened to dream and compared to illusion and so on;
To illustrate the total transformation,
To space it is likened, to gold and water and so on.

The verses distinguishing phenomena and pure being composed by the guardian Maitreya are herewith concluded.

The Kashmiri Khenpo Mahadzana and the Tibetan translator Lotsawa Gelong Senge Gyaltsen collaborated in translating this [from Sanskrit into Tibetan] and in correcting their work, thus providing this finalized version.

DISTINGUISHING WISDOM AND APPEARANCE
BY MIPHAM JAMYANG NAMGYAL

The Commentary

༄། ཆོས་དང་ཆོས་ཉིད་རྣམ་པར་འབྱེད་པའི་
ཚིག་ལེའུར་བྱས་པའི་འགྲེལ་པ་
ཡེ་ཤེས་སྣང་བ་རྣམ་འབྱེད་བཞུགས་སོ།

།རྣམ་པར་མི་རྟོག་ཡེ་ཤེས་རྡོ་རྗེ་ཡིས།
།གཟུང་འཛིན་རི་བོ་རབ་ཏུ་བཅོམ་མཛད་པས།
།བསམ་གྱིས་མི་ཁྱབ་ཡེ་ཤེས་སྐུ་བརྙེས་པ།
།སྟོན་མཆོག་ཐུབ་པ་དེ་ལ་ཕྱག་འཚལ་ལོ།
།གང་གི་ཟབ་ཅིང་རྒྱ་ཆེའི་ཆོས་ཀྱི་མཛོད།
།འཛིན་མཛད་རྒྱལ་བའི་སྲས་པོ་འཇམ་པའི་དབྱངས།
།རྒྱལ་ཚབ་ས་བཅུའི་དབང་ཕྱུག་མ་ཕམ་པའི།
།ཞབས་སེན་ནོར་བུ་གཙུག་གི་རྒྱན་དུ་བཏེན།
།གང་འདིར་ཐེག་པ་ཆེན་པོའི་ཆོས་ཀྱི་མཛོད།
།ཀུན་གྱི་ནང་ན་སྙིང་པོར་གྱུར་པ་ཡི།
།རྣམ་པར་མི་རྟོག་ཡེ་ཤེས་ཟབ་མོའི་དོན།
།གསལ་མཛད་བསྟན་བཅོས་ཆེན་པོའི་རྣམ་བཤད་བྱ།

Distinguishing Wisdom and Appearance
A Commentary on the Stanzas
Distinguishing Phenomena and Pure Being

The Author's Introduction

To the one who has conquered the mountain, perceived and perceiver,
With the vajra, original nonconceptual wisdom,
Thus gaining the inconceivable wisdom body;
To the Teacher Supreme, the Mighty Sage, I bow.

The Heir of the Victor, Manjushri, as well as The Regent—
The tenth-level Lord, the Invincible Maitreya—
Hold the treasures of Dharma both vast and profound.
The nails of their feet are the jewels I support as my crown.

That which will here be explained is the glorious shastra
Elucidating profound reality—
Original nonconceptual wisdom, the heart
Of Mahayana Dharma's abundance of treasures.

།དེ་ཡང་རྒྱལ་བའི་སྲས་པོ་འཕགས་པ་ཐོགས་མེད་ཀྱིས་མི་ལོ་བཅུ་གཉིས་སུ་རྗེ་བཙུན་བྱམས་པ་བསྒྲུབས་པའི་མཐར་ཞལ་མངོན་སུམ་དུ་བསྟན་ནས་དགའ་ལྡན་ལྷའི་གནས་སུ་ཁྲིད་དེ། རྒྱལ་བའི་བཀའ་ཐམས་ཅད་ཀྱི་དགོངས་པ་འགྲེལ་པའི་བསྟན་བཅོས་རྒྱན་གཉིས་འབྱེད་གཉིས་རྒྱུད་བླ་མ་སྟེ་ཆོས་ལྔ་བསྟན་པ་འདི་ལ། མཁས་པ་ཁ་ཅིག་གིས་ལྔ་ཀ་བསྟན་བཅོས་དཀྱུས་གཅིག་གི་ཚུལ་དུ་བཞེད་ལ། ཡང་ཁ་ཅིག་གིས་ཐེག་གསུམ་དང་ཐེག་གཅིག་ངེས་དོན་དུ་བཤད་པ་སོགས་མཐར་ཐུག་གི་བསྟན་བྱ་མི་མཐུན་པས་བསྟན་བཅོས་ཀྱི་ལུས་གཅིག་ཏུ་འདོད་པ་དེ་བཀག་ནས། རང་ལུགས་བཀའ་སོ་སོའི་དགོངས་འགྲེལ་དུ་བཞེད་ལ། དེ་ལ་ཡང་ཐོག་མཐའ་གཉིས་དབུ་མ་དང་། བར་མ་གསུམ་སེམས་ཙམ་གྱི་དགོངས་འགྲེལ་དུ་བཞེད་པ་དང་། མདོ་རྒྱན་ཁོ་ན་སེམས་ཙམ་གྱི་གཞུང་དང་། གཞན་བཞི་དབུ་མར་བཞེད་པ་དང་། མངོན་རྟོགས་རྒྱན་དབུ་མ་དང་།

གཞན་བཞི་སེམས་ཙམ་དུ་བཞེད་པ་དང་། ཡང་ཁ་ཅིག་གིས་ལྔ་ཀ་སེམས་ཙམ་གྱི་དགོངས་པར་གནས་པ་དང་། ཡང་ལྔ་ཀ་དབུ་མའི་དགོངས་པར་གནས་པར་བཞེད་པ་སོགས་ཡོད་ཀྱང་། དོན་ལ་མངོན་རྟོགས་རྒྱན་ནི་བཀའ་བར་པ་ཤེས་རབ་ཀྱི་ཕ་རོལ་ཏུ་ཕྱིན་པའི་དགོངས་འགྲེལ་དང་། རྒྱུད་བླ་མ་འཁོར་ལོ་ཐ་མའི་ངེས་དོན་བདེ་གཤེགས་སྙིང་པོ་བསྟན་པའི་མདོ་རྣམས་ཀྱི་དགོངས་འགྲེལ་དུ་རྩོད་པ་མེད་པར་གྲུབ་ཅིང་། དེ་གཉིས་ཀས་མཐར་ཐུག་གི་རིགས་གཅིག་དང་ཐེག་པ་གཅིག་ཏུ་འདོད་ལ་དབུ་མའི་དོན་དུ་དགོངས་པ་མཐུན་པ་ཉིད་དོ། །

That heir of the Victor, the noble Asanga, performed the practice of the beloved master of loving kindness, Maitreya, for what—measured in human time—would be twelve years, at the end of which he beheld him face to face. As a result he was transported to Tushita,[1] where he was presented with five works. These include the two Ornaments, the two Distinctions, and *Buddha Nature*,[2] which are treatises serving as commentaries on the intention of all levels of the teaching of the Victor.

There are some scholars who see all five as forming a single coordinated work. Others refute this assertion on the grounds that, in the interpretation provided by their tradition, these treatises disagree in their presentation of the ultimate on such points as there being one or three vehicles from the perspective of the definitive meaning. They therefore consider them to be distinct commentaries representing different ways of clarifying the intent of the Buddha's teaching. That is to say, some take the first and last as commentaries on the thought of the Madhyamaka and the middle three as applying to the Chittamatra.[3] There are also some who consider *The Ornament of the Sutra Collection* alone to be a work of the Chittamatra, the other four to be Madhyamaka. There are some who consider *The Ornament of Direct Realization* to be Madhyamaka, the other four Chittamatra; others who locate all five within the thinking of the Chittamatra; and others still who consider all five to belong to the Madhyamaka, and so on.

What can, nevertheless, be indisputably established is that *The Ornament of Direct Realization* is in fact a commentary on the intent of the middle level of the teaching of the Buddha, the Prajnaparamita;[4] and that *Buddha Nature* is a commentary on the purport of the sutras presenting the sugatagarbha[5] and belongs to the definitive meaning associated with the final turning. Both of these texts propose but one family[6] and one vehicle ultimately, which is in accord with the thinking of the Madhyamaka.

མདོ་སྡེ་རྒྱན་ནི་སྡུ་མ་དེ་གཉིས་ཀྱིས་བཤད་བྱའི་མདོ་ལས་གཞན་པའི་མདོ་སྡེ་ཕལ་མོ་ཆེའི་དོན་ཕྱོགས་གཅིག་བསྡེབས་པའི་དགོངས་འགྲེལ་ཡིན་ལ། དེར་རིགས་དང་ཐེག་པ་གཅིག་ཏུ་མ་ངེས་པར་བསྟན་པ་སོགས་ཕལ་ཆེར་སེམས་ཙམ་གྱི་མདོ་སྡེའི་དགོངས་པ་གཙོ་བོར་འགྲེལ་པར་གསལ་ལོ། །

འབྱེད་གཉིས་པོ་འདི་ནི་ཐེག་པ་སྤྱི་ཡི་རྒྱ་ཆེ་བ་དང་ཟབ་མོའི་ཕྱོགས་སྟོན་པར་བྱེད་པ་སྟེ། འདི་དག་ཏུ་རང་བཞིན་གསུམ་དང་ཕྱི་དོན་མ་གྲུབ་པའི་ཚུལ་རྒྱ་ཆེར་སྟོན་ཀྱང་དེ་ཙམ་ཞིག་གིས་སེམས་ཙམ་པའི་གཞུང་ཁོ་ནར་འགྱུར་བའི་ངེས་པ་མེད་དེ། དབུ་མའི་དགོངས་པ་ཡང་ཆོས་སྐད་དེ་དག་གི་ཚུལ་གྱིས་བཞག་པ་ཙམ་ལ་འགལ་བ་མེད་པ་ནི།

ལང་གཤེགས་ལས།

།ཆོས་ལྔ་རང་བཞིན་གསུམ་དང་ནི།
།རྣམ་པར་ཤེས་པའི་ཚོགས་བརྒྱད་དང་།
།བདག་མེད་དོན་གྱི་རྣམ་གཉིས་པོར།
།ཐེག་ཆེན་མཐའ་དག་བསྡུས་པ་ཡིན།

ཞེས་ཆོས་སྐད་འདི་དག་ཐེག་ཆེན་མཐའ་དག་གི་སྤྱི་སྡོམ་དུ་གསུངས་པ་དང་། ཡུམ་གྱི་དགོངས་པ་གསལ་བར་བྱེད་པའི་མདོ་བྱམས་ཞུས་ན་ཡང་ངོ་བོ་ཉིད་གསུམ་གྱི་ཆོས་སྐད་

The Ornament of the Sutra Collection differs from the two texts just mentioned with respect to the sutra topics it explains. It is a commentary which compiles the topics of the majority of the sutras in a single volume. On the whole, such factors as its lacking a decisive presentation of the single family and vehicle clearly indicate it to be primarily a commentary on the thought of the sutras associated with the Chittamatra.

The two Distinctions teach the vast as well as the profound dimensions of the [Mahayana] vehicle in general, and even though these extensively teach the three natures[7] and the sense in which outer objects do not exist, this in itself does not limit them to being works of the Chittamatra. There is no contradiction in saying that such Dharma terminology equally applies to the thinking of the Madhyamaka. In *The Sutra from the Journey to Srilanka* such terms are taught as general headings applicable to the whole of the Mahayana, as follows:

> The five prevailing themes[8] and natures three
> Along with the eightfold collection of consciousness[9]
> And the pith in the two forms of lack of self-entity—
> These are found throughout the Mahayana.

This is also explicitly illustrated by *The Sutra Requested by Maitreya* which clarifies the intent of The Mother[10] [and is therefore a text of the Madhyamaka], where such Dharma terms as "the three essentials"[11] are taught

འདི་དག་བསྟན་པ་སོགས་ཀྱིས་དངོས་སུ་གསལ་ལ། སེམས་ཙམ་པའི་འདོད་གཞུང་བཞིན་གཉིས་སྟོང་གི་ཤེས་པ་བདེན་གྲུབ་ཏུ་མི་འདོད་འོས་མེད་ཀྱི་ཚིག་ཟིན་དང་རིགས་པ་གང་ཡང་མི་སྣང་བས་ན། ཕྱོགས་སུ་མ་ལྷུང་བར་ཐེག་པ་སྤྱི་ཡི་དགོངས་འགྲེལ་དུ་བཤད་པ་ལ་ཉེས་པ་ཅི་ཡང་མེད་པར་མ་ཟད་གཞུང་གི་བབ་དེ་ལྟར་གནས་པས་ན་དབུས་མཐའ་རྣམ་འབྱེད་འདི་ཐེག་པ་གསུམ་གྱི་ལམ་རྒྱ་ཆེ་བའི་རྣམ་བཞག་སྟོན་པའི་གཞུང་དང་། ཆོས་ཉིད་རྣམ་འབྱེད་འདི་བདེན་གཉིས་ཟུང་འཇུག་དབུ་མ་རྣལ་འབྱོར་སྤྱོད་པའི་ཚུལ་དང་མཐུན་པར། ཟབ་མོའི་མདོ་སྡེ་ཀུན་གྱི་བརྗོད་བྱའི་སྙིང་པོ་རྣམ་པར་མི་རྟོག་པའི་ཡེ་ཤེས་གཏན་ལ་འབེབ་པའི་གཞུང་ཡིན་ལ། དེའི་ཕྱིར་ཤིན་ཏུ་ཟབ་པས་ན་འདི་དང་རྒྱུད་བླ་གཉིས་བཀའ་རྒྱ་དམ་པའི་ཚུལ་གྱིས་རྒྱ་གར་དུའང་ཕྱིས་སུ་དཔེ་རྒྱུན་མ་བྱུང་བའི་ཚེ་མངའ་བདག་མཻ་ཏྲི་པས་མཆོད་རྟེན་ཞིག་གི་སེར་ཀ་ནས་འོད་བྱུང་བ་གཟིགས་པ་དེ་ནས་ཆོས་ཉིད་རྣམ་འབྱེད་དང་རྒྱུད་བླ་མ་གཉིས་ཀྱི་དཔེ་ཕྱུང་སྟེ་སྤར་འཕེལ་བ་ཡིན་པས། ཞ་མ་ལོ་ཙཱ་བ་སེངྒེ་རྒྱལ་མཚན་གྱིས་ཆོས་ཉིད་རྣམ་འབྱེད་ཀྱི་དཔེ་འདི་འགྱུར་ཞུས་མཛད་པའི་ཚེ། པཎྜིཏས་ཤོག་ལྷེབ་རེ་རེ་བཞིན་གནང་ནས་འདི་ཆུད་མ་ཟོས་པར་གྱིས། དཔེ་བཀའ་དམ་པས་རྒྱུན་དཀོན་ཕྱིར་འདི་མེད་སོང་ན་རྗེ་བཙུན་བྱམས་པ་འཛམ་བུའི་གླིང་དུ་སྐུ་མྱ་ངན་ལས་འདས་པ་ཡིན་ནོ། །ཞེས་གཙིགས་སུ་མཛད་པར་གསུངས་པ་ལྟར།

without there being a single categorical statement or logical argument which would necessarily amount to asserting true existence for the consciousness empty of duality as this is asserted in the works of the Chittamatra.

Not only is there no error whatsoever in classifying the two Distinctions as commentaries not falling into any specific school of the Mahayana but applying to the whole vehicle in general; they even follow the same pattern of explanation found in the major works of other vehicles. *Distinguishing the Middle from the Extremes* is thus a text which teaches the vast aspect of the paths of all three vehicles; and *Distinguishing Pure Being*[12] provides rigorous understanding of nonconceptual original wisdom, the very essence of the subject matter found in all sutra collections treating of the profound and does so in a manner that corresponds to the way the Yogacharamadhyamaka[13] teaches the union of the two truths.

It is precisely for this reason, and due to their extraordinary profundity, that the manuscripts of *Distinguishing Phenomena and Pure Being* and *Buddha Nature* were bound with a seal of secrecy during the Indian period and later in that period disappeared from circulation. That is when the mighty lord Maitripa, on discovering light emerging from a crack in a stupa, extracted the manuscripts of both these texts and disseminated them anew.

That is also why, during the time when Shama Lotsawa Senge Gyaltsen was studying this present work and preparing his translation of it, his learned teacher[14] emphasized its significance by giving him only one page at a time with the admonition, "Beware that no harm befalls this! It is a text rarely available, because it is bound with a seal. Its disappearance would be tantamount to the body of the beloved master of loving kindness, Maitreya, passing from this world."

ལྷ་བའི་རིས་གསང་སྟོན་པའི་ཟབ་དོན་ཡིན་པས་ཐེག་པ་ཆེན་པོ་པ་ཀུན་གྱིས་ལྷ་བ་འདི་ལྟར་རྟོགས་དགོས་པས་དབུ་སེམས་སུ་ཡི་ལུགས་སུ་བཀྲལ་ཀྱང་མི་རུང་བ་མེད་མོད། དཔེར་ན་ཤེར་ཕྱིན་གྱི་མདོ་སྡེ་ལ་དབུ་སེམས་ཀྱི་སློབ་དཔོན་རྣམས་ཀྱིས་སོ་སོ་རང་རང་གི་བཞེད་གཞུང་དུ་བཀྲལ་ཀྱང་གཞུང་དེའི་དགོངས་པ་མཐར་ཐུག་དབུ་མར་གནས་པ་ལྟར། བཞུང་འདི་ཡང་སེམས་ཙམ་གྱི་ལྟར་སྟོན་པའི་བསྟན་བཅོས་སུ་བཞེད་མཁན་ཡང་། རང་བློའི་རྒྱལ་དང་སྦྱར་ཏེ་དེ་ལྟར་བཤད་ཀྱང་འགལ་བ་མེད་ལ། འོན་ཀྱང་དོན་དུ་གཞུང་འདིས་ཐེག་པ་ཆེན་པོའི་ཟབ་དོན་མཐར་ཐུག་པ་རྣམ་པར་མི་རྟོག་པའི་ཡེ་ཤེས་ཉིད་ཅི་ལྟ་བུ་ཡིན་པ་གསལ་བར་སྟོན་པས་ན། ཟབ་མོའི་མདོ་སྡེ་མཐའ་དག་གི་སྤྱི་འགྲེལ་དུ་འགྲོ་ཞིང་། ཀུན་རྫོབ་ཆོས་ཅན་གྱི་འདོད་ཚུལ་སེམས་ཙམ་དང་མཐུན་ལ། དོན་དམ་ཆོས་ཉིད་ཀྱི་འདོད་ཚུལ་དབུ་མ་དང་མཐུན་པས་མཐར་ཐུག་གི་དགོངས་པ་དབུ་མར་གནས་ཤིང་དབུ་སེམས་ཟུང་འཇུག་གི་ཚུལ་གྱིས་ཐེག་པ་ཆེན་པོའི་ལྟ་བའི་གནད་སྟོན་པའི་ཚུལ་དུ་གོ་ཞིང་བཤད་ན་བསྟན་བཅོས་ཆེན་པོའི་དགོངས་པ་གཏིང་ཕྱིན་པར་བཤད་པར་འགྱུར་རོ། །

Since what it teaches is profound reality, which is the critical secret hidden within the view, and because the realization of such a view is required of all practitioners of the Mahayana, there is no incongruity in interpreting it from the perspective of either the Madhyamaka or the Chittamatra systems.

Nevertheless, even given that such texts as the Prajnaparamita sutras are interpreted in the works of individual Chittamatrin and Madhyamika preceptors in accordance with their own respective schools, the ultimate intention of these texts is still that of the Madhyamaka. Similarly, even though there are scholars in whose treatises this present work is interpreted according to the Chittamatra, since this is relevant to a specific level of understanding, there is no contradiction in explaining it thus; nevertheless, it is in fact a work which clearly portrays the character of nothing less than nonconceptual original wisdom, the point of the utmost profundity within the Mahayana, for which reason it serves as a commentary applicable in general to any sutra treating of the profound.

Since it accords with the Chittamatra in the form its assertions take with respect to the phenomenal world,[15] which constitutes apparent reality, and since it accords with the Madhyamaka in its interpretation of pure being, which constitutes genuine reality, it demonstrates the key points of Mahayana view in a fashion which unites Chittamatra and Madhyamaka, while its ultimate purport rests with the Madhyamaka. To understand and explain it in this way covers the entire range of implication afforded by this great treatise.

༄། །དེ་ལྟ་བུའི་བསྟན་བཅོས་ཆེན་པོ་འདི་འཆད་པ་ལ། མཚན་དོན། འགྱུར་ཕྱག །གཞུང་དོན། མཇུག་དོན་བཞི། དང་པོ།

རྒྱ་གར་སྐད་དུ། དྷརྨ་དྷརྨཏཱ་བི་བྷཾ་ག་ཀཱ་རི་ཀཱ། བོད་སྐད་དུ། ཆོས་དང་
ཆོས་ཉིད་རྣམ་པར་འབྱེད་པའི་ཚིག་ལེའུར་བྱས་པ།

རྒྱ་གར་སྐད་དུ་དྷརྨ། བོད་སྐད་དུ་ཆོས། དེ་བཞིན་དུ་སྦྱར་ཏེ་དྷརྨཏཱ་ཆོས་ཉིད། བི་བྷཾ་ག །རྣམ་པར་འབྱེད་པ། ཀཱ་རི་ཀཱ་ཚིག་ལེའུར་བྱས་པ་ཞེས་པ་སྟེ། ཆོས་ཅན་འཁོར་བ་དང་ཆོས་ཉིད་མྱ་ངན་ལས་འདས་པའི་རང་བཞིན་ཇི་ལྟ་བུ་ཡིན་པ་མ་ནོར་བར་སྟོན་ཅིང་རྣམ་པར་འབྱེད་པའི་མཚན་དེ་སྐད་དུ་བསྟན་པའོ། །

གཉིས་པ།

མགོན་པོ་བྱམས་པ་ལ་ཕྱག་འཚལ་ལོ།

འགྲོ་བ་ཐམས་ཅད་ཀྱི་མགོན་པོ་ཉིད་དུ་གྱུར་པ། བྱམས་པ་ཆེན་པོ་དང་ལྡན་པའི་ཡོན་ཏན་གྱི་སྒོ་ནས་བྱང་ཆུབ་སེམས་དཔའི་གནས་སྐབས་ནས་སངས་རྒྱས་ཀྱི་བར་དུ་བྱམས་པ་ཞེས་པའི་མཚན་གྱི་གྲགས་པ་མི་འདོར་བ་སྐྱེ་བ་གཅིག་གིས་ཐོགས་པའི་བྱང་ཆུབ་སེམས་དཔའ་ཆེན་པོ་ད་ལྟ་དགའ་ལྡན་ན་བཞུགས་པ་གཞུང་འདི་ཉིད་མཛད་པ་པོ་དེ་ལ་ལོ་ཙྪ་བ་དག་གིས་འགྱུར་མཛད་པའི་ཐོག་མར་སྒོ་གསུམ་གུས་པ་ཆེན་པོས་ཕྱག་འཚལ་ལོ་ཞེས་བརྗོད་པར་མཛད་པ་ཡིན་ནོ། །

The explication of the treatise

I. The meaning of the title
II. The translators' homage
III. The main body of the text
IV. The concluding statement

I. The meaning of the title

In Sanskrit: dharmadharmatavibhagakarika
In Tibetan: chos dang chos nyid rnam par 'byed pa'i tshig le'ur byas pa

What *in Sanskrit* is called *dharma* or *in Tibetan chos*, in English is "phenomena." Similarly, *dharmata* or *chos nyid* means "pure being," *vibhaga* or *rnam par 'byed pa* means "distinguishing," with *karika* or *tshig le'ur byas pa* meaning "rendered in stanzas of verse."

This title conveys the sense of accurately depicting the basic character of the phenomenal world of samsara and the nature of pure being, i.e., nirvana, in a manner wholly consistent with the way they actually are and distinguishing between them.

II. The translators' homage

To the guardian Maitreya we bow in supplication.

Here the translators pay homage in the following words: "From the outset, with great respect and through all three gateways, *we bow in supplication to the* author of this present work, the great bodhisattva presently residing in Tushita, that *guardian* of all sentient beings without exception who is renowned as *Maitreya* because of his natural gift of great loving kindness.[16] He has been known by this name for as long as he has been a Bodhisattva and will continue to bear this name even when he attains buddhahood, from which he is hindered by one birth only."

གསུམ་པ་ལ། བསྟན་བཅོས་རྩོམ་པ་ལ་འཇུག་པའི་ཡན་ལག་དང་། བརྩམ་བྱ་བསྟན་

བཅོས་ཀྱི་ལུས་དངོས་གཉིས་ལས། དང་པོ་ལ་ཚིགས་སུ་བཅད་པ་གཅིག་སྟེ།

ཤེས་ནས་གང་ཞིག་ཡོངས་སུ་སྤང་བྱ་ཞིང་།
གཞན་འགའ་ཞིག་ནི་མངོན་སུམ་ཉིད་དུ་བྱ།
དེས་ན་དེ་དག་མཚན་ཉིད་རྣམ་དབྱེ་བ།
བྱེད་པར་འདོད་ནས་བསྟན་བཅོས་འདི་བརྩམས་སོ།

ཤེས་ནས་གང་ཞིག་ཡོངས་སུ་སྤང་བར་བྱ་བ་འཁོར་བ་ཉིད་ཡིན་ཞིང་། དེ་ལས་གཞན་དུ་གྱུར་པ་འགའ་ཞིག་ནི་མངོན་སུམ་ཉིད་དུ་བྱ་བ་ཡིན་ཏེ་གང་ཞེ་ན་མྱ་ངན་ལས་འདས་པའོ། །

དེས་ན་སློབ་མ་རྣམས་ཀྱིས་ཤེས་ཤིང་སྤང་བླང་དུ་བྱ་བའི་དངོས་པོ་ནི་འདི་ཙམ་དུ་ཟད་པས་ན་འཁོར་འདས་དེ་དག་གི་མཚན་ཉིད་ཇི་ལྟ་བུ་ཡིན་པ་ཕྱིན་ཅི་མ་ལོག་པའི་ཚུལ་གྱིས་རྣམ་པར་དབྱེ་བ་བྱེད་པར་འདོད་ནས་འཕགས་པ་བྱམས་པ་བདག་གིས་བསྟན་བཅོས་ཆེན་པོ་འདི་ཤེས་རབ་དང་སྙིང་རྗེ་ཆེན་པོས་བརྩམས་སོ། །ཞེས་གསུངས་སོ། །

III. The main body of the text

A) The verse introducing the author's intention in composing this treatise
B) The actual body of the treatise

A) The verse introducing the author's intention

Something there is to be given up fully through knowing
And something else which can only be actualized,
Because of which this treatise has been composed
With the wish to distinguish the traits defining these.

There is something, namely, samsara itself, which is *to be given up fully through knowing,* and *something else* quite different from this, which *can* only *be actualized* directly.[17] If you ask what the latter might be, it is nirvana.

These constitute fully and precisely the substance of what is to be known and respectively relinquished and adopted by gifted beings, *because of which this* great *treatise has been composed* with precise knowledge and great compassion by the noble Maitreya *with the wish to distinguish the traits defining these*—i.e., samsara and nirvana—in an unmistaken manner corresponding precisely to the way they are.

གཉིས་པ་ལ། མདོར་བསྟན་པ་དང༌། རྒྱས་པར་བཤད་པ་དང༌། མཚོན་པའི་དཔེས་མཇུག་བསྡུ་བ་གསུམ། དང་པོ་ལ། ངོ་བོ་ངོས་བཟུང༌། དེའི་མཚན་ཉིད་སོ་སོར་བཤད། དེ་དག་གྲུབ་པའི་ཚུལ། དེ་གཉིས་གཅིག་ཐ་དད་བརྟག་པ་བཞི། དང་པོ།

འདི་དག་ཐམས་ཅད་མདོར་བསྡུ་ན།
རྣམ་པ་གཉིས་སུ་ཤེས་བྱ་སྟེ།
ཆོས་དང་དེ་བཞིན་ཆོས་ཉིད་ཀྱིས།
ཐམས་ཅད་བསྡུས་པ་ཉིད་ཕྱིར་རོ།
དེ་ལ་ཆོས་ཀྱིས་ཕྱེ་བ་ནི།
འཁོར་བ་ཡིན་ཏེ་ཆོས་ཉིད་ཀྱིས།
རབ་ཏུ་ཕྱེ་བ་ཐེག་གསུམ་གྱི།
མྱ་ངན་ལས་ནི་འདས་པའོ།

གསུང་རབ་ཀྱི་བརྗོད་བྱ་འདི་དག་ཐམས་ཅད་མདོར་བསྡུ་ན་རྣམ་པ་གཉིས་སུ་ཤེས་པར་བྱ་སྟེ་གང་ཞེ་ན། ཆོས་དང་དེ་བཞིན་དུ། ཆོས་ཉིད་ཞེས་བྱ་བ་འདི་གཉིས་ཡིན་ལ། དེ་གཉིས་ཀྱིས་ཤེས་བྱའི་གནས་ཐམས་ཅད་བསྡུས་པ་ཉིད་ཡིན་པའི་ཕྱིར་འདི་གཉིས་ལེགས་པར་གཏན་ལ་ཕབ་ན་གསུང་རབ་ཀྱི་བརྗོད་བྱ་མཐའ་དག་ལ་མ་རྨོངས་པར་འགྱུར་རོ། །

B) The actual body of the treatise

1 The brief presentation
2 The expanded explanation
3 The concluding summary employing examples to illustrate the point

1 The brief presentation

I) The points comprising the essential subject matter
II) The defining traits of each of these
III) The rationale underlying these traits
IV) Examining both for sameness and difference

I) The points comprising the essential subject matter

A summary of everything in brief
Should be known to include the following two motifs,
Since everything can be summarized fully in terms
Of phenomena together with pure being.

That which is classified here as phenomena
Is samsara; that which is classified precisely
As pure being is nirvana, transcendence of grief,
As this is defined by the vehicles, which are three.

A summary of everything expressed in the scriptures *should be known in brief to include the two motifs, phenomena together with pure being, since everything* included under topics of knowledge *can be summarized fully in terms of* these two. Consequently, once a firm understanding of these two has been acquired, one will no longer be ignorant of any subject expressed in the scriptures.

དེ་ལ་སྐབས་འདིར་ཆོས་ཀྱིས་རབ་ཏུ་ཕྱེ་བ་ནི་གཟུང་འཛིན་གཉིས་སུ་སྣང་བ་ཅན་གྱི་འཁོར་བ་ཡིན་ཏེ། ཐར་པ་དང་རྣམ་མཁྱེན་འདོད་པ་རྣམས་ཀྱིས་འཁྲུལ་བའི་སྣང་ཚུལ་གང་གི་རང་བཞིན་ཤེས་པར་བྱ་བ་དང་སྤང་བར་བྱ་བའི་གཞིར་གྱུར་པའི་ཆོས་རྣམས་འདི་ཙམ་དུ་ཟད་པའི་ཕྱིར་རོ། །

ཆོས་ཉིད་ཀྱིས་རབ་ཏུ་ཕྱེ་བ་ནི་ཐེག་པ་གསུམ་གྱི་མྱ་ངན་ལས་འདས་པ་ཡིན་ཏེ། ཇི་ལྟར་སྣང་བའི་འཁོར་བ་འདི་ལ་གང་ཟག་གི་བདག་དང་། ཆོས་སུ་གྲུབ་པའི་ངོ་བོ་ཉིད་མེད་པར་མཐོང་བའི་སྟོབས་ཀྱིས་གནས་ཡོངས་སུ་གྱུར་པའི་མྱང་འདས་ཐོབ་པ་ནི་གནས་ཚུལ་ལ་ཡང་དག་པར་ཞུགས་པས་གནས་སྣང་མི་མཐུན་པ་མེད་པའི་ཕྱིར་ཡང་དག་པར་ཤེས་པར་བྱ་བ་དང་མངོན་དུ་བྱ་བ་ནི་འདི་ཙམ་དུ་ཟད་པའོ། །

That which is specifically *classified here* in this context *as phenomena is samsara,* meaning the realm of manifestation, which consists of a duality of perceived and perceiver, because there is no other base for what is to be known and relinquished by those aspiring to liberation and omniscience than phenomena, whose makeup consists of this deluded mode of appearance.

Pure being is that which is classified precisely as being *nirvana as this is defined by the vehicles* of *which* there *are three,* because it is the attainment of a *transcendence of grief* which is a complete transformation. This transformation is brought about by virtue of seeing that, in samsara—in whatever form it may appear—there is no personal self and no essential component comprising phenomena. Since this is authentic resting in the fundamental mode of being, there is no discrepancy here between being and manifestation. This is all that there is to be correctly understood; there is nothing more to actualize.

གཉིས་པ་ལ་ཆོས་ཀྱི་མཚན་ཉིད་དང་། ཆོས་ཉིད་ཀྱི་མཚན་ཉིད་གཉིས། དང་པོ།

དེ་ལ་ཆོས་ཀྱི་མཚན་ཉིད་ནི།
གཉིས་དང་ཇི་ལྟར་མངོན་བརྗོད་པར།
སྣང་བ་ཡང་དག་མ་ཡིན་པའི།
ཀུན་རྟོག་པ་སྟེ་མེད་སྣང་ཕྱིར།
དེས་ན་ཡང་དག་མ་ཡིན་ནོ།
དེ་ཡང་ཐམས་ཅད་དོན་མེད་ཅིང་།
རྟོག་ཙམ་ཡིན་པས་ཀུན་རྟོག་པའོ།

བཤད་མ་ཐག་པ་དེ་ལ་ཆོས་ཞེས་བརྗོད་པ་འཁོར་བ་དེ་ཉིད་ཀྱི་མཚན་ཉིད་ནི། གཟུང་འཛིན་གཉིས་སུ་སྣང་བ་དང་། ཇི་ལྟར་སྣང་བ་དེ་ལ་དེ་དང་དེ་ལྟར་ཞེན་ཅིང་མིང་སྣ་ཚོགས་ཀྱིས་མངོན་པར་བརྗོད་པར་སྣང་བ་ཅན་འདི་ཉིད་དེ། འདི་ལྟར་རྒྱུ་བཞིན་ཁྲིས་པའི་རི་མོ་ལ་མཐོ་དམན་མེད་ཀྱང་ཡོད་པར་སྣང་བ་ལྟར་གཟུང་འཛིན་གཉིས་སུ་སྣང་བ་དེ་ནི། སྣང་བ་ལྟར་དོན་ལ་མ་གྲུབ་པས་ན་དཔེར་ན་སྐྲ་ཤད་ལ་སོགས་པར་སྣང་བ་བཞིན་དུ་ཡང་དག་མ་ཡིན་པའི་རང་གི་ཀུན་ཏུ་རྟོག་པ་ཙམ་སྟེ། ཡུལ་མེད་བཞིན་ཏུ་སེམས་ལ་སྣང་བའི་ཕྱིར་རོ། །

II) The defining traits of each of these

A) The definition of phenomena
B) The definition of pure being

A) The definition of phenomena

Here the traits of phenomena are defined
As duality plus assumption and formulation,
Whose appearance is the mistaken conceptual process,
Since what appears is not and is thus not real.
No referents have ever existed either
And, being but concept, consist of conceptualization.

In line with the immediately preceding explanation, *the traits of* samsara itself, *here* called "*phenomena*," *are defined as* the realm of manifestation, which consists of appearances involving a *duality* of perceived and perceiver *plus* the *assumption* that anything appearing in such a way actually exists in that way; this is accompanied by *formulation,* which applies terminology.

This is comparable to a well-composed painting in which there appears to be a background and a foreground, even though there is none. The dualistic *appearance* of perceived and perceiver *is* merely one's own *mistaken conceptual process, since what appears* to the mind, namely the object, *is not* existent—even while it appears. This is illustrated by such examples as the strands of hair which appear to a victim of cataracts,[18] because these do not exist as the objects they appear to be.

དེས་ན་གཉིས་སུ་སྣང་བ་དེ་ནི་སྣང་ངོར་ཡོད་ཀྱང་དོན་ལ་ཡང་དག་མ་ཡིན་པའོ། །

དེའི་ཕྱིར་གཉིས་སུ་སྣང་བ་དེ་ལ་བརྟེན་ནས་ནང་གི་ཡིད་ཀྱིས་འདི་དང་འདི་ཞེས་མངོན་པར་བརྗོད་ཅིང་གདགས་པ་དེ་ཡང་རྣམ་པ་ཐམས་ཅད་ནས་ཐམས་ཅད་དུ་བརྗོད་བྱའི་དོན་དུ་གྲུབ་པ་མེད་ཅིང་། རང་གི་རྟོག་པས་བཏགས་པ་ཙམ་ཡིན་པས་ཆོས་སུ་བརྗོད་པ་ཇི་སྙེད་པ་ནི་ཀུན་ཏུ་རྟོག་པ་ཙམ་དུ་གྲུབ་པའོ། །

མདོར་བསྡུ་ན། གཉིས་སྣང་དང་གཉིས་ཞེན་གྱི་ཆོས་ཐམས་ཅད་ཀུན་བཏགས་ཙམ་ལས་རང་གི་ངོ་བོ་ཉིད་མེད་བཞིན་སྣང་བར་བསྟན་ཏོ། །

གཉིས་པ།

གཞན་ཡང་ཆོས་ཉིད་མཚན་ཉིད་ནི།
གཟུང་བ་དང་ནི་འཛིན་པ་དང་།
བརྗོད་པར་བྱ་དང་རྗོད་པར་བྱེད།
ཁྱད་མེད་དེ་བཞིན་ཉིད་ཡིན་នོ།

གཞན་ཡང་ཆོས་ཉིད་ཀྱི་མཚན་ཉིད་ནི་གོང་ལས་བཟློག་སྟེ། གཟུང་བ་དང་ནི་འཛིན་པ་གཉིས་སུ་སྣང་བ་དང་། དེ་ལ་ཞེན་ནས་བརྗོད་པར་བྱ་བ་དང་། རྗོད་པར་བྱེད་པའི་ཐ་སྙད་ཀྱིས་ཁྱད་པར་དུ་བྱར་མེད་པ་སོ་སོ་རང་གིས་རིག་པར་བྱ་བའི་ཡུལ་དེ་བཞིན་ཉིད་ཡིན་ནོ། །

Thus, anything whose appearance involves this duality, even though existing in an apparent sense, *could not be real* in actual fact.

For this reason, *no referents* of the terms used *have ever existed either* in any way or at any time which the inner rational mind could formulate or to which it could assign some specific name on the basis of the dualistic appearance. *Being but* an imputation on the part of one's own *concept*s, the complex manifold referred to as phenomena *consist*s solely *of* this *conceptual process*.

To sum up what has been said here, all phenomena, which are composed of dualistic appearance to which dualistic assumption is added, are nothing other than complete imputations having no existence with an actual constituent of their own, while nevertheless appearing.

B) The definition of pure being

The other factor, pure being, is defined
As suchness, in which there is no differentiation
Between a factor perceived and a perceiver,
A signifier contra a signified.

The other factor is *pure being*, which is *defined as* the opposite of the above; i.e., it involves *no* process of *differentiation between* a *perceiver* and a *perceived* appearing to be two and *a signified* referent *contra a signifier* in the form of the conventions employed based on the dualistic assumption. It is *suchness*, the object of intimate and detailed self-aware wisdom.

གསུམ་པ་དོན་ལ་མེད་བཞིན་དུ་སྣང་བ་དེ་ལྟ་བུ་ཡིན་པའི་འཐད་པ་ཉེ་བར་བསྒྲུབ་པ་ནི།

མེད་པ་སྣང་ཕྱིར་འཁྲུལ་པ་ནི།
ཀུན་ནས་ཉོན་མོངས་རྒྱུ་ཡིན་ཏེ།
སྒྱུ་མའི་གླང་ཆེན་སོགས་སྣང་ཞིང་།
ཡོད་པའང་སྣང་བ་མིན་ཕྱིར་རོ།
མེད་སྣང་དག་ལས་གང་རུང་ཞིག
མེད་ན་འཁྲུལ་དང་མ་འཁྲུལ་དང་།
དེ་བཞིན་ཀུན་ནས་ཉོན་མོངས་དང་།
རྣམ་པར་བྱང་བ་མི་འཐད་དོ།

དངོས་པོའི་དོན་ལ་དེ་ལྟར་མེད་པ་ཡིན་བཞིན་དུ་སྣང་བའི་ཕྱིར་འཁྲུལ་པའི་སྣང་བ་རབ་རིབ་ལྟ་བུ་དེ་ནི་ཀུན་ནས་ཉོན་མོངས་པ་ཐམས་ཅད་འབྱུང་བའི་རྒྱུ་ཡིན་ཏེ། གཉིས་སུ་སྣང་བ་ལ་བརྟེན་ནས་གཉིས་སུ་ཞེན་པ་སྐྱེ་ལ། དེ་ལ་བརྟེན་ནས་བག་ཆགས་སྣ་ཚོགས་འབྱུང་བའི་ཕྱིར་རོ། །

དེ་ཡང་དཔེ་ཇི་ལྟར་ན་རྫས་སྔགས་ཀྱི་སྟོབས་ལས་མེད་བཞིན་ཏུ་སྒྱུ་མའི་གླང་ཆེན་གྱི་གཟུགས་དང་རྨི་ལམ་དུ་བུད་མེད་བཟང་མོ་སོགས་སྣང་བ་བཞིན་དུ། ཆོས་འདི་དག་ཀྱང་མེད་བཞིན་ཏུ་སྣང་ཞིང་དེའི་དབང་གིས་གནས་ལུགས་སུ་ཡེ་ནས་ཡོད་པ་བདག་མེད་གཉིས་ཀྱི་དོན་གང་ཡིན་པ་དེའང་སོ་སོའི་སྐྱེ་བོ་ལ་སྣང་བ་མིན་པའི་ཕྱིར་རོ། །

III) The rationale underlying these traits

This third point presents the logical grounds validating the lack of objective existence of that which nevertheless appears.

> *Because what does not exist appears, delusion*
> *Provides the cause for completely afflicted states;*
> *Since things like illusory elephants appear,*
> *Even what does exist does not appear.*
> *If either the lack of existence or the appearance*
> *Were missing, delusion and freedom from delusion*
> *And likewise states afflicted in every respect*
> *And thorough refinement would be unjustified.*

All appearances are delusive in the same way as those associated with cataracts, *because* things *do not* actually *exist* as they *appear,* even while they are appearing. This *delusion provides the cause for* the occurrence of all *states* which are *afflicted in every respect,* because it is on the basis of there appearing to be a duality that the dualistic assumption is entertained, and it is on such a basis that the various tendencies are formed.

Furthermore, these phenomena, which do not exist and yet appear, prevent *what **does** exist* from the outset—namely, the abiding nature, the freedom from the two forms of self—*from appearing* to ordinary beings. This could be illustrated by such examples as beautiful women in dreams and *things like* the forms of *illusory elephants,* which do not exist apart from the hypnotic influence of an illusionist's materials and charms but nevertheless *appear.*

ཇི་སྐད་བཤད་པ་དེ་ལྟ་བུ་ཡིན་པ་དེའི་ཕྱིར་འཁོར་འདས་དང་འཁྲུལ་གྲོལ་འཐད་ཀྱི་གཞན་དུ་དེ་དག་འཐད་པར་མི་འགྱུར་ཏེ། དོན་དུ་མེད་པ་དང་མེད་བཞིན་སྣང་བ་གཉིས་པོ་ཟུང་དུ་ཚོགས་པ་དེ་ལྟ་བུ་མིན་པར་དེ་གཉིས་ལས་གང་རུང་ཞིག་མེད་ན་འཁྲུལ་པ་དང་མ་འཁྲུལ་བ་དང་དེ་བཞིན་དུ་ཀུན་ནས་ཉོན་མོངས་པ་དང་རྣམ་པར་བྱང་བ་ཞེས་བྱ་བ་གཉིས་ཡོད་པར་རྣམ་པ་ཀུན་ཏུ་མི་འཐད་པར་འགྱུར་ཏེ། དོན་ལ་མེད་པ་མ་ཡིན་པར་གཉིས་སུ་སྣང་བ་ལྟར་ཡོད་ཅིང་གྲུབ་ན་དེ་ལྟར་འཛིན་པ་དེ་འཁྲུལ་པའམ་ཕྱིན་ཅི་ལོག་ཏུ་མི་འཐད་ལ། འཁྲུལ་པ་དེ་ལས་བཟློག་པའི་ཐབས་མེད་པས་མྱང་འདས་ཀྱང་རྣམ་པ་ཀུན་ཏུ་མེད་པར་འགྱུར་རོ། །

དོན་ལ་མེད་པ་ལྟར་སྣང་བ་ཡང་མེད་ན་སུ་ཡང་གཟུང་འཛིན་གྱི་འཁྲུལ་པ་ཅན་དུ་འགྱུར་མི་སྲིད་པས་ཀུན་ཉོན་གཞི་མེད་པར་འགྱུར་ལ། དེ་མེད་པས་དེ་ལས་ལྡོག་པ་རྣམ་བྱང་ཞེས་བྱ་བའང་མེད་པར་འགྱུར་ཏེ་རི་བོང་གི་རྭ་མེད་པ་ལ་བཅད་དུ་མེད་པ་བཞིན་ནོ། །

དེས་ན་མེད་སྣང་ཟུང་དུ་ཚོགས་པ་དེའི་ཕྱིར་མེད་པ་ལ་ཡོད་པར་འཛིན་པའི་འཁྲུལ་པ་ལ་ཀུན་ཉོན་ཕྱོགས་སྲིད་ཅིང་། མེད་པ་ལ་མེད་པར་ཤེས་པའི་སྒོ་ནས་མ་འཁྲུལ་བའི་ལམ་གྱིས་ཐོབ་པའི་མྱང་འདས་ཀྱང་སྲིད་པ་ཡིན་ནོ། །

Because it is as just explained, there are logical grounds for asserting samsara and nirvana, delusion and liberation; otherwise these would be unjustifiable.

If there were no such complementary relationship, that is, *if either* of these two, *the lack of* objective *existence or the appearance* of the nonexistent, *were missing,* both *delusion and freedom from delusion and likewise states afflicted in every respect as well as* their *thorough refinement would be unjustified* in every sense.

If, on the one hand, there were no lack of objective existence but the duality of perceived and perceiver existed and were verifiably present as it appears, to perceive it in that way could not be justified as delusion or a distortion, in which case delusion would not be reversible by any means and nirvana would be excluded in every respect.

If, on the other hand, the appearance of something which does not really exist did not manifest, it would not be possible for anyone to entertain the delusion of perceived and perceiver, as a result of which there would be no basis for complete affliction. Since affliction would not exist, neither would its reversal, designated "the process of refinement," just as the nonexistent horns of a rabbit cannot be clipped.

One must, therefore, conclude that there is a complementary relationship between the lack of existence and the appearance, such that, on the one hand, the delusion of perceiving what does not exist as existing as well as the related afflictive factors become possible; and on the other, nirvana is also possible and can be attained through a path on which delusion is eliminated by knowing the nonexistent to be nonexistent.

བཞི་པ།

གཉིས་པོ་དག་ནི་གཅིག་ཉིད་དང་།
སོ་སོ་བ་ཡང་མ་ཡིན་ཏེ།
ཡོད་པ་དང་ནི་མེད་པ་དག
ཁྱད་པར་ཡོད་དང་མེད་ཕྱིར་རོ།

འཁོར་འདས་སམ་ཆོས་དང་ཆོས་ཉིད་གྲགས་པ་གཉིས་པོ་དག་ནི་ངོ་བོ་གཅིག་པ་ཉིད་དང་ངོ་བོ་སོ་སོ་བ་ཡང་མ་ཡིན་ཏེ། ཇི་ལྟར་ན་ཆོས་ཉིད་རང་བཞིན་གྱིས་རྣམ་པར་དག་པའི་མྱང་འདས་ནི་གནས་ལུགས་སུ་ཡེ་ནས་ཡོད་པ་དང་ནི། ཆོས་ཅན་འཁོར་བའི་ཆོས་གཉིས་སུ་སྣང་བ་རྣམས་ནི་སྣང་བ་ལྟར་གནས་ལུགས་སུ་མེད་པ་དག་གི་ཁྱད་པར་ཡོད་པའི་ཕྱིར་ཐ་སྙད་དུ་དེ་གཉིས་གཅིག་མ་ཡིན་པ་དང་། གཅིག་མེད་ན་གཅིག་ཤོས་ཀྱང་མེད་པའམ་ཡང་དག་པར་ན་ཆོས་ཉིད་ནི་ཆོས་ཅན་དེ་དག་མ་གྲུབ་པ་ཙམ་གྱིས་རབ་ཏུ་ཕྱེ་བ་ལས་གཞན་ཐ་དད་དུ་མེད་པས། ཡོད་པ་ཆོས་ཉིད་དང་མེད་པ་ཆོས་ཅན་གྱི་ཁྱད་པར་ནི་ལྟོས་ཏེ་བླང་དོར་ཕྱེ་བ་ཙམ་ལས། དོན་ཐ་དད་པར་གྲུབ་པའི་ངོ་བོ་ཉིད་ཙུང་ཟད་ཀྱང་མེད་པའི་ཕྱིར་ཐ་དད་པའང་མ་ཡིན་པར་རིག་པར་བྱ་བ་ཉིད་དུ་འགྱུར་རོ། །

IV) Examining both for sameness and difference

These two are not one and the same nor do they differ,
Because, between that which exists and that which does not,
A distinction exists and yet does not exist.

These two, known as samsara and nirvana or phenomena and pure being, *are not one and the same* in essence *nor do they differ* in essence. How is that to be understood?

They are not the same conventionally, *because a distinction exists between* pure being and the phenomenal world. Pure being, naturally pure nirvana, is *that which exists* from the beginning as the abiding nature. The phenomenal world, with its dualistic appearances that make it samsara, is *that which does not* exist in reality as appears to be the case.

And *yet,* it should be understood that they *are not* separate for the following reasons:

- If the one did not exist, its counterpart would not either.
- Strictly speaking, pure being, other than being distinguishable from the phenomenal world as its mere lack of verifiable existence, does not exist separately.
- The distinction between the existent, pure being, and the nonexistent, the phenomenal world, is relative, being a differentiation merely with respect to what is to be adopted and what is to be rejected; other than that, there is not even the slightest existence of an actual essence constituting these as separate entities.

གཉིས་པ་རྒྱས་པར་བཤད་པ་ལ། ཆོས་རྒྱས་པར་བཤད་པ་དང་། ཆོས་ཉིད་རྒྱས་པར་བཤད་པ་གཉིས་ལས། དང་པོ་ལ་སྡོམ་དུ་བསྟན་པ་དང་། སོ་སོར་བཤད་པ་གཉིས། དང་པོ།

> རྣམ་པ་དྲུག་གིས་ཆོས་དག་ལ།
> འཇུག་པ་བླ་ན་མེད་པ་སྟེ།
> མཚན་ཉིད་དང་ནི་གྲུབ་པ་དང་།
> གཅིག་དང་ཐ་དད་མ་ཡིན་ཞིང་།
> གནས་ནི་ཐུན་མོང་ཐུན་མོང་མིན།
> གཟུང་དང་འཛིན་པར་སྣང་བ་ནི།
> མེད་ལ་རབ་ཏུ་འཇུག་པས་སོ།

ཞེས་པར་བྱ་བའི་ཚུལ་རྣམ་པ་དྲུག་གིས་ཐོས་བསམ་གྱི་སྒོ་ནས་ཆོས་དག་ལ་འཇུག་པ་ནི་ཆོས་དེ་དག་གཏན་ལ་འབེབས་ཚུལ་བླ་ན་མེད་པ་ཡིན་པ་སྟེ། གང་གིས་ན་སྤྱང་བྱ་འཁོར་བའི་ཆོས་ཀྱི་རང་བཞིན་དེ་དག་འཇུག་ཚུལ་འདི་ལྟ་བུས་མ་ལུས་པ་བདེ་བླག་ཏུ་གཏན་ལ་འབེབས་ནུས་པའི་ཕྱིར་རོ། །

འཇུག་པའི་ཚུལ་དྲུག་པོ་དེ་གང་ཞེ་ན། འཁོར་བའི་ཆོས་ཀྱི་མཚན་ཉིད་ཇི་ལྟ་བུ་ཡིན་པ་ཤེས་པར་བྱ་བ་ལ་འཇུག་པ་དང་ནི། དེའི་མཚན་ཉིད་དེ་ལྟར་གྲུབ་པའི་ཚུལ་ལ་འཇུག་པ་བསྟན་པ་དང་། ཆོས་དང་ཆོས་ཉིད་དེ་དག་གཅིག་དང་ཐ་དད་མ་ཡིན་པའི་ཚུལ་ཤེས་

2 The expanded explanation

I) The expanded explanation of phenomena
II) The expanded explanation of pure being

I) The expanded explanation of phenomena

A) A presentation of the headings
B) An explanation of each of these

A) A presentation of the headings

Because it provides a thorough introduction
To their characteristics as well as their rationale,
Their neither being the same nor different,
The ground in common and not in common shared,
And the lack of appearance involving perceiver-perceived,
This sixpoint approach to phenomena is the best.

This approach to phenomena by way of a listening and reflection which apply the following *six point* method to the subject matter *is the best* way of establishing a reliable guideline for understanding phenomena, because *it provides* a thorough introduction which enables one to easily understand the makeup of all samsaric phenomena, the factor to be relinquished.

For those who inquire, the six ways of approaching this are as follows:

- The approach which involves knowing precisely how the *characteristics* of samsara, or phenomena, are defined
- The approach in which the *rationale* behind such defining characteristics is demonstrated
- The approach entailing knowledge of the sense in which phenomena and pure being are *neither the same nor different*

པར་བྱ་ཞིང་འཇུག་པ་དང་། འཁོར་བ་དེ་ཡི་གནས་ནི་ཐུན་མོང་བ་ཤེས་པར་བྱ་བ་ལ་འཇུག་པ་དང་། ཐུན་མོང་མིན་པའི་ཚུལ་ཤེས་པ་ལ་འཇུག་པ་དང་། གཟུང་བ་དང་འཛིན་པར་སྣང་བ་དེ་ནི་མེད་པའི་དོན་ལ་རབ་ཏུ་འཇུག་པའི་ཚུལ་ཤེས་པ་དང་དྲུག་གི་སྒོ་ནས་བསྟན་པས་དེའི་དོན་ཁོང་དུ་ཆུད་པར་నུས་སོ། །

གཉིས་པ་སྟོམ་གྱི་དོན་སོ་སོར་བཤད་པ་ལ། དང་པོ་གསུམ་བཤད་ཟིན་པར་བསྟན་པ་དང་། ཕྱི་མ་གསུམ་སྐབས་འདིར་བཤད་པའོ། །དང་པོ།

དེ་ལ་མཚན་ཉིད་གྲུབ་པ་དང་།
གཅིག་དང་ཐ་དད་མ་ཡིན་པ།
ཇི་ལྟར་མདོར་བསྟན་བཞིན་དུའོ།

འཇུག་པ་དྲུག་པ་བསྟན་པ་དེ་ལ་མཚན་ཉིད་དང་གྲུབ་པ་དང་གཅིག་དང་ཐ་དད་མ་ཡིན་པ་གསུམ་ནི་གོང་དུ་ཇི་ལྟར་མདོར་བསྟན་གྱི་སྐབས་སུ་བཤད་པ་བཞིན་དུ་ཤེས་པར་བྱའོ། །

- The approach involving knowledge of samsara's *common ground*
- The approach involving knowledge of the forms of experience *not shared in common*
- *A thorough introduction* to the reality where the *appearance involving perceived-and-perceiver* duality is *lack*ing

Because phenomena are presented in terms of these six forms of knowledge, it is possible to comprehend their meaning.

B) An explanation of each of these

(1) A passing reference to the first three points
(2) An explanation of the last three points

(1) A passing reference to the first three points

Of these, the defining traits and the rationale,
As well as the lack of sameness and difference,
Are just as these were demonstrated in brief.

Of these six approaches presented, there are three, *the defining traits, the rationale, as well as the lack of sameness and difference,* which should be understood *just as these have been demonstrated in brief* in the section explained above.

གཉིས་པ་ལ། གནས་གཉིས་པོ་བཤད་པ་དང་། གཟུང་འཛིན་མེད་པའི་དོན་ལ་འཇུག་ཚུལ་བཤད་པ་གཉིས། དང་པོ་ལ་ཐུན་མོང་དུ་མདོར་བསྟན། སོ་སོའི་དོན་རྒྱས་པར་བཤད་པ་གཉིས། དང་པོ།

གང་ཞིག་གང་དུ་འཁོར་བ་ན།
དེ་ནི་ཀུན་ཏུ་གནས་པ་སྟེ།
སེམས་ཅན་ཁམས་དང་སྣོད་ཀྱི་ཁམས།
སྣོད་ཀྱི་ཁམས་ནི་ཐུན་མོང་ལྟར།
རྣམ་པར་རིག་པ་ཐུན་མོང་ཡིན།
སེམས་ཅན་ཁམས་ནི་ཐུན་མོང་དང་།
ཡང་ན་ཐུན་མོང་མ་ཡིན་པའོ།

སེམས་ཅན་གྱི་ཁམས་གང་ཞིག་སྣོད་ཀྱི་ཁམས་གང་དུ་སྐྱེ་བ་ལེན་པའི་ཚུལ་གྱིས་ཡང་ནས་ཡང་དུ་འཁོར་བའི་གནས་སྐབས་ན། སེམས་ཅན་གྱི་འཇིག་རྟེན་དང་སྣོད་ཀྱི་འཇིག་རྟེན་དུ་གྲགས་པའི་འཇིག་རྟེན་རྣམ་པ་གཉིས་པོ་དེ་ནི་ཀུན་ཏུ་འཁོར་བར་བྱ་བའི་གནས་སུ་གྲགས་པ་སྟེ། འདི་ལྟར་བརྟེན་པ་སེམས་ཅན་གྱི་ཁམས་དང་རྟེན་སྣོད་ཀྱི་ཁམས་གཉིས་པོ་འདི་ལས་གཞན་པའི་འཁོར་བའི་གནས་བྱ་བ་ཅི་ཡང་མེད་དོ། །

(2) An explanation of the last three points

(I) The explanation of the two types of ground

(II) How to approach the reality free of perceived and perceiver

(I) The explanation of the two types of ground

(A) A brief presentation of both in common

(B) An expanded explanation of the meaning of each

(A) A brief presentation of both in common

As long as there is someone circling somewhere,
These are the grounds in each and every case—
The constituents of beings and those of the vessel.
The constituents of the vessel appear to be shared,
The awareness being the common experience;
Some of the constituents of beings
Are experienced in common and some are not.

As long as there is someone with the constituents belonging to a sentient being *circling,* in the sense of repeatedly taking rebirth *somewhere* within the constituents of the vessel, *these* two kinds of world, known as the world of sentient beings and the world of the vessel, *are* designated as *the grounds* for the enactment of the samsaric cycle *in each and every case.* There is nothing whatsoever that could be named as the grounds for samsara other than these two, *the constituents of* sentient *beings* as that which is supported *and* the constituents *of the vessel* as the support.

དེ་ལ་ཐུན་མོང་བ་དང་ཐུན་མིན་དེ་དག་གང་ཞེ་ན། སྣོད་ཀྱི་འཇིག་རྟེན་གྱི་ཁམས་འདི་དག་ནི་བག་ཆགས་མཐུན་པར་སད་པའི་འགྲོ་བ་ལ་ཐུན་མོང་ལྟར་སྣང་ཞིང་དེ་ལྟར་རྣམ་པར་རིག་པའམ་ཤེས་པར་བྱ་བ་ཉིད་ཀྱི་ཆ་ནས་གནས་ཐུན་མོང་བ་ཞེས་བྱ་བ་ཡིན་ནོ། །

སེམས་ཅན་གྱི་ཁམས་ཀྱིས་བསྡུས་པའི་ཆོས་ལ་ནི་འགའ་ཞིག་ཐུན་མོང་པར་གྱུར་པ་དང་། ཡང་ན་འགའ་ཞིག་ཐུན་མོང་མ་ཡིན་པར་གྱུར་པའང་ཡོད་པའོ། །

གཉིས་པ་གནས་ཐུན་མོང་བ་བཤད་པ་དང་། ཐུན་མིན་བཤད་པའོ། །དང་པོ།

དེ་ཡང་སྐྱེ་དང་ཐ་སྙད་དང་།
རྗེས་སུ་གཟུང་དང་ཚར་གཅོད་དང་།
ཕན་པ་དང་ནི་གནོད་པ་དང་།
ཡོན་ཏན་སྐྱོན་ནི་ཕན་ཚུན་དུ།
བདག་པོ་ཉིད་ཀྱིས་ཕན་ཚུན་རྒྱུ།
ཡིན་པའི་ཕྱིར་ན་ཐུན་མོང་པའོ།

སེམས་ཅན་གྱི་ཁམས་ཀྱིས་བསྡུས་པའི་ཆོས་ལ་ཐུན་མོང་དུ་གྱུར་པ་དེ་ཡང་ཇི་ལྟར་བཞག་ཅེ་ན། མངལ་ནས་སྐྱེ་བ་དང་། ལུས་དང་ངག་གི་ཐ་སྙད་རྣམ་པར་རིག་པར་བྱེད་པ་དང་།

One might ask here, "What is a matter of collective experience and what is not?" *The constituents* of the world *of the vessel* are referred to as *the common* ground of *experience* in the sense that—for beings whose operative tendencies correspond—they *appear* in a seemingly *common* fashion and there is a corresponding *awareness* or consciousness of them. Regarding the phenomena comprising *the constituents of* sentient *beings,* there *are* some that are *experienced in common and* some that are *not.*

(B) An expanded explanation of the meaning of each

1) Experience comprising a common ground
2) Experience not shared in common

1) Experience comprising a common ground

Further, birth and conventions, to nurture, subdue,
Benefit, harm, excellent features, and faults
Are mutually caused by way of an interchange,
Because of which these are experience shared in common.

If one asks for a *further* classification specifying which phenomena comprising the constituent features of sentient beings are experienced in common, included would be *birth* from a womb; the *conventions* of body and speech conveying symbolic expression;[19] the case of one party *nurtur*ing or

གཞན་གྱིས་གཞན་རྗེས་སུ་བཟུང་དང་། ཚར་གཅོད་པ་དང་། ཕན་འདོགས་པ་དང་ནི་གནོད་པ་བྱེད་པ་དང་། ཅིག་ཤོས་ལ་བརྟེན་ནས་ཐོས་སོགས་ཀྱི་ཡོན་ཏན་སྐྱེ་བ་དང་། ཆགས་སོགས་ཀྱི་སྐྱོན་འབྱུང་བ་རྣམས་ནི་དེར་སྣང་བའི་རྣམ་ཤེས་སྐྱེ་བ་ལ་སེམས་ཅན་གཅིག་ལ་གཅིག་ཕན་ཚུན་དུ་བདག་པོ་ཡི་རྐྱེན་དུ་གྱུར་པ་ཉིད་ཀྱིས་ཕན་ཚུན་རྒྱུ་བྱེད་པ་ཡིན་པའི་ཕྱིར་ན་འདི་དག་ནི་སྣང་གྱུར་ཐུན་མོང་བ་ཞེས་བྱའོ། །

དེ་ལ་སྐྱེ་བ་ཐུན་མོང་དུ་གྱུར་ཚུལ་ནི། རང་གི་ལས་ཀྱིས་རྒྱུ་བྱས་ཕ་མ་གཉིས་ཀྱི་ས་བོན་ལས་ལྷན་ཅིག་བྱེད་རྐྱེན་བྱས་པའི་རྒྱུ་ཐུན་མོང་བ་དེས་འབྲས་བུ་མངལ་ནས་སྐྱེས་པའི་ལུས་འགྲུབ་པ་ལྟ་བུའོ། །

ཐ་སྙད་ཐུན་མོང་བ་ནི་གཞན་གྱི་ལུས་ངག་གི་རྣམ་པར་རིག་བྱེད་ཀྱིས་བསྐུལ་ནས། གཞན་ལྟ་བ་དང་སྨྲ་བ་སོགས་ལ་འཇུག་པ་ལྟ་བུའོ། །

དེ་བཞིན་དུ་གཅིག་གིས་གཅིག་ཆོས་དང་ཟང་ཟིང་གི་སྒོ་ནས་རྗེས་སུ་བཟུང་བ་དང་ཤག་འགྱེད་པ་དང་གཡུལ་སྤྲོད་པ་སོགས་ཀྱིས་ཚར་གཅོད་པ་དང་། འཇིགས་པ་ལས་བསྐྱབས་པ་སོགས་ཀྱིས་ཕན་འདོགས་པ་དང་། བརྡུང་བརྡེག་སོགས་གནོད་པ་བྱེད་པ་དང་ཐོས་པ་སོགས་ཀྱི་སྒོ་ནས་ཡོན་ཏན་སྐྱེད་པ་དང་། ལྟ་ངན་བསྟན་པ་དང་ཆགས་པ་སོགས་བསྐྱེད་པས་སྐྱོན་ཅན་དུ་བྱས་པ་རྣམས་ནི་ཕ་རོལ་པོས་བདག་རྐྱེན་བྱས་ཤིང་རང་གི་རྒྱུད་ཀྱི་ཆོས་ཀྱི་རྒྱུའི་གཙོ་བོ་བྱས་ཏེ་འབྲས་བུ་ཐུན་མོང་བ་གཅིག་གྲུབ་པའི་ཆ་ནས་ཐུན་མོང་

*subdu*ing another; the case of providing *benefit* or producing *harm;* the development of *excellent qualities,* such as those associated with listening and so on which come about in conjunction with reliance on another, as do the occurrence of such *faults* as attachment and so on. These forms of consciousness *are* called appearances whose *experience* is *shared in common, because* their occurrence in each instance is *mutually caused by way of* an *inter*mediate condition enabling an ex*change* between sentient beings.

Specifically, the way in which birth is a case of collective experience is in the sense that the *cause* deriving from the karmic actions of the one to be born combines with the simultaneously active *conditions* in the form of the seed and egg of the parents to produce a common cause through which the result, a body born from a womb, is produced. Conventions are shared in common in the sense that one follows specific social customs,[20] engages in conversation, and so on, animated by the symbolic expressions associated with the bodies and speech of others.

These and similar cases of exchanges where one party, for example, nurtures another with the Dharma or with material goods; subdues another in various ways ranging from verbal contest to engaging in combat; provides for another's benefit by protecting them from frightening circumstances and so on; produces harm through various forms of physical violence; gives rise to positive qualities through such means as listening to teachings; induces faults in another through encouraging attachment and the like or through teaching wrong views and so on. These are all cases that are called "common" from the perspective of there being a specific common result produced through the combination of the primary cause deriving from the phenomena of one mindstream and the intermediate condition deriving from those of another.

པ་ཞེས་བྱ་སྟེ། ཐ་སྙད་དུ་རྒྱུ་རྐྱེན་དེ་དག་ཚོགས་པས་འབྲས་བུ་དེ་དག་བསྐྱེད་པ་ཡིན་ཀྱང་། དོན་ལ་བདག་པོའི་རྒྱུ་ཞེས་སྨོས་པས་རྣམ་པར་རིག་པ་ལས་གཞན་པའི་དམིགས་རྐྱེན་དུ་གྱུར་པ་ཕྱི་དོན་མ་གྲུབ་པ་དང་། ཕྱི་སྣོད་སོགས་ཐུན་མོང་བ་ལྟར་སྣང་བ་རྣམས་ཀྱང་ནང་གི་རྣམ་པར་རིག་པའི་གཟུང་ཆ་ཙམ་ལས་གཞན་དུ་མེད་པས་ཐུན་མོང་བའི་ཕྱི་དོན་མ་གྲུབ་པར་བསྟན་པའང་ཡིན་ནོ། །

གཉིས་པ།

གནས་དང་རྣམ་པར་རིག་པ་དང་།
བདེ་སྡུག་ལས་དང་འཆི་འཕོ་དང་།
སྐྱེ་བ་དང་ནི་བཅིངས་པ་དང་།
གྲོལ་བ་ཐུན་མོང་མ་ཡིན་ཕྱིར།
དེ་གནས་ཐུན་མོང་མ་ཡིན་པའོ།

གནས་ཀུན་གཞི་རྣམ་པར་ཤེས་པ་དང་། རྣམ་པར་རིག་པ་ཚོགས་བདུན་དང་། སོ་སོའི་བདེ་སྡུག་མྱོང་བ་དང་། སེམས་པས་ལས་བསགས་པ་དང་། འཆི་འཕོ་བ་དང་། སོ་སོའི་སྲིད་པར་སྐྱེ་བ་ལེན་པ་དང་ནི། འཁོར་བར་བཅིང་བ་དང་། འཁོར་བ་ལས་གྲོལ་བ་རྣམས་ནི་རང་གི་རྒྱུད་ཀྱི་ཆོས་ཐུན་མོང་མ་ཡིན་པ་ཡིན་པའི་ཕྱིར། སོ་སོའི་རྒྱུད་ཀྱི་མྱོང་གྱུར་ཐུན་མིན་དེ་དག་སེམས་ཅན་གཞན་དང་ཐུན་མོང་དུ་བྱར་མི་བཏུབ་པས། དེ་རྣམས་ནི་སེམས་ཅན་གྱི་གནས་ཐུན་མོང་མ་ཡིན་པ་ཞེས་བྱའོ། །

It is valid to state that, in a conventional sense, such results are produced through the combination of such causes and conditions. In actual fact, however, the term "intermediate condition" indicates that outer referents perceived in common do not verifiably exist. This is because there are no outer referents existing extrinsic to image-awareness[21] which could serve as the focal condition, and because the appearances seemingly experienced in common as the outer vessel and so on are nothing other than the perceived aspect of the inner awareness.

2) Experience not shared in common

Since the ground and awareness, happiness, suffering,
Action, transition at death, captivity, birth,
And liberation are not observed in common,
They comprise the realm of experience not shared in common.

Since the ground, the all inclusive base consciousness; the principles of *awareness,* i.e., the sevenfold collection; personal experience of *happiness* and *suffering;* mentally committed karmic *actions*; *transition at death;* taking re*birth* in a specific form of conditioned existence; the *captivity* or bondage experienced in the samsaric cycle; *and liberation* from that cycle *are* all phenomena of an individual mindstream which are *not observed in common*, and since these are the private experiences belonging to an individual mindstream and cannot be rendered directly accessible to common experience on the part of other sentient beings, *they comprise the realm of experience* designated "*not shared in common*" with others.

དྲུག་པ་ལ། ཕྱི་རོལ་གཟུང་བ་མེད་པར་རྣམ་པར་རིག་པ་ཙམ་གྱིས་གྲུབ་མཐའ་བསྟན་པ་དང་། དེ་ལས་གཟུང་འཛིན་མེད་པའི་དོན་ལ་འཇུག་ཚུལ་གཉིས། དང་པོ་ལ་འཛིན་པ་ལས་ཐ་དད་པའི་གཟུང་བ་མེད་པར་བསྟན་པ་དང་། དེ་ལ་མ་ངེས་པ་སྤང་བའོ། །དང་པོ།

ཕྱི་རོལ་གཟུང་བ་ཐུན་མོང་བར།
སྣང་བ་འཛིན་པའི་རྣམ་རིག་པའོ།
རྣམ་པར་ཤེས་ལས་ཕྱི་རོལ་དུ།
གྲུར་པའི་དོན་ཡོད་མ་ཡིན་ཏེ།
ཐུན་མོང་བ་ཉིད་ཡིན་ཕྱིར་རོ།

ཕྱི་དོན་ལ་མངོན་པར་ཞེན་པ་རྣམས་འདི་སྐམ་དུ་བལྟ་བྱ་ཐུན་མོང་བའི་རི་ལ་སོགས་པ་རྟལ་དུ་གྲུབ་པ་རྣམས་འདི་ལྟར་བསྐྱོན་མེད་དུ་ཡོད་པའི་ཕྱིར་ཕྱི་དོན་གྲུབ་པོ་སྙམ་ན་དེ་མ་ཡིན་ཏེ། ཕྱི་རོལ་གྱི་གཟུང་བ་གང་ཞིག་ཐུན་མོང་བར་སྣང་བ་རི་ལ་སོགས་པ་ཆོས་ཅན། ནང་གི་ཤེས་པ་ལས་ཐ་དད་པའི་ཕྱི་དོན་བེམ་པོའི་ངོ་བོར་གྲུབ་པ་མེད་དེ། བག་ཆགས་མཐུན་པར་སད་པ་རྣམས་ཀྱི་ནང་གི་འཛིན་པའི་རྣམ་པར་རིག་པ་ཉིད་ཕྱི་རོལ་གྱི་དོན་དེ་དང་དེའི་རྣམ་པར་སྣང་བ་ཡིན་པའི་ཕྱིར། དཔེར་ན་སྨྱི་ལམ་གྱི་གཟུགས་ལྟ་བུའོ། །

(II) How to approach reality, which is free of perceived and perceiver

(A) The tenet stating that there is no outer referent, only image-awareness

(B) The resultant procedure for approaching reality, the freedom from perceived and perceiver

(A) The tenet stating that there is no outer referent, only image-awareness

1) The lack of a perceived object discrete from the perceiver

2) The elimination of any further uncertainty

1) The lack of a perceived object discrete from the perceiver

What appear to be outer, perceivable in common,
Are perceiving awareness; they are not referents
Existing as something extrinsic to consciousness,
Because they are only experienced as common.

Those who cling compulsively to the existence of outer objects claim, "Outer objects exist, because no one can deny that anything composed of atoms, such as mountains and any other object observed in common, exists." But that is not how it is.

Given *what appear to be outer* and *perceivable in common,* such as mountains and so on, as the postulated subject, these are not outer referents discrete from the inner consciousness and existing with a material essence, because they *are* the inner *perceiving awareness* itself appearing as the image of this and that outer referent for those whose operative habitual tendencies correspond, just like forms in a dream.

དེའི་ཕྱིར་ན་རྣམ་པར་ཤེས་པ་ལས་གཞན་པ་ཕྱི་རོལ་དུ་གྱུར་པའི་དོན་ཡོད་པ་མ་ཡིན་ཏེ། འདི་ལྟར་བལྟ་བྱ་ཐུན་མོང་བའི་ཕྱི་དོན་ཞེས་བྱ་བ་དེ་ཡང་། རྒྱུད་མི་གཅིག་པའི་འགྲོ་བ་དུ་མ་ལ་ཐུན་མོང་དུ་སྣང་བ་ཉིད་ཡིན་པའི་ཕྱིར་སོ་སོའི་རྒྱུད་ཀྱི་འཛིན་པ་ལས་ཐ་དད་དུ་མེད་པ་ཉིད་དུ་གྲུབ་པར་འགྱུར་རོ། །

དེའི་རྒྱུ་མཚན་ཇི་ལྟ་བུ་ཞེ་ན་ཕྱི་དོན་གྲུབ་པའི་སྒྲུབ་བྱེད་དུ་བཀོད་པའི་བལྟ་བྱ་ཐུན་མོང་བ་ཤེས་བྱ་བ་དེ་ནི། རྒྱུད་སོ་སོའི་ངོ་སྐལ་ལ་སྣང་ལུགས་འདྲ་བ་ཙམ་ཞིག་གིས་ཐུན་མོང་བའི་ཕྱི་དོན་ཞེས་འཛོག་པར་ཟད་ན་སྣང་བ་དེ་དག་ནི་རང་རང་སོ་སོའི་རྒྱུད་ཀྱི་སྣང་བ་ཡིན་གྱི་ཐུན་མོང་བ་ནམ་ཡང་མི་སྲིད་ལ། སྣང་བ་ཙམ་དེ་ལས་གཞན་པའི་ཕྱི་དོན་ཞེས་པ་ཐུན་མོང་བ་ཞིག་ནི་འདི་འོ་ཞེས་རིགས་པས་ནམ་ཡང་བསྟན་མི་ནུས་ཏེ་སེམས་ལ་སྣང་བ་ལས་ཡུལ་དེ་ཡོད་པར་འཛོག་དགོས་ཀྱི། མ་སྣང་བར་ནི་འཇལ་བྱེད་ཚད་མ་མེད་པས་ན་འཛོག་མི་རིགས་སོ། །

དེས་ན་བལྟ་བྱ་ཐུན་མོང་བ་ཞེས་པ་འདི་ལ་ལེགས་པར་བརྟགས་ན་ཐུན་མོང་བ་ཞེས་སུ་འཛོག་པའི་རྒྱུ་མཚན་རྒྱུད་སོ་སོའི་སྣང་བ་འདྲ་བས་འཛོག་ན། སྣང་བ་དེ་ནི་འདྲ་བ་ཡིན་ནའང་། དེའི་རྒྱུ་ཕྱི་དོན་ཐུན་མོང་བ་གཅིག་ངེས་པར་གྲུབ་མི་དགོས་ཏེ། སྒྱུ་མའི་སྔགས་ཀྱིས་མིག་བསླད་པའི་སྐྱེ་བོ་རྣམས་ལ་སྣང་བ་མཐུན་པར་འཆར་བ་བཞིན། བག་ཆགས་མཐུན་པར་སད་པའི་སྐྱེ་བོ་རྣམས་ལ་བག་ཆགས་དེའི་ནུས་པ་མ་ཟད་ཀྱི་རིང་ལ་

What are being called "outer objects observed in common" *are not referents existing as something extrinsic to* or other than *consciousness, because they are only* apparently *experienced as common* by a variety of beings whose mindstreams are not identical. But this is what proves that they are nothing other than differing perceptions of differing mindstreams.[22]

And how does it prove that? What are claimed to be "factors observed in common" are proposed as providing the proof for the existence of outer referents. But these can only be posited as "outer referents experienced in common" due to a similarity in the character of their appearance from the subjective viewpoint of distinct mindstreams. But that means these appearances are the private impressions of mindstreams which differ among themselves. And that means they could never constitute common experience.

Thus to say, "There are outer objects which are something other than a mere appearance (or impression)" and to say, "Here is one experienced in common" could never be demonstrated logically, since, to do so, one would have to posit the existence of objects other than those which appear to a mind. But it would make no sense to posit an object that could not appear to any mind, since it could not be evaluated through valid cognition.

On subjecting this so-called "common experience" to critical scrutiny, the reason for claiming it to be "common" turns out to be built on the similarity of appearance with respect to mindstreams which themselves differ, so it follows that, even though there is a similarity in the appearance, its underlying cause includes no necessity of a specific outer common referent literally existing, just as corresponding appearances manifest for spectators under the influence of the charms of an illusionist. Similarly, for creatures whose operative habitual tendencies correspond, not only will environments and so on have a similar appearance for as long as the energy of those habitual tendencies has not been exhausted, but, what is more, the specific

གནས་ལ་སོགས་པ་འདྲ་བར་སྣང་ན་ཡང་། འདྲ་བར་སྣང་བའི་རྒྱུ་གཅིག་ཕྱི་རོལ་ན་དོན་དུ་གྲུབ་པ་མེད་དེ་ཆུ་གཅིག་ལའང་ལས་སྣང་ཐ་དད་པའི་འགྲོ་བ་དྲུག་གི་མཐོང་སྣང་ཐ་དད་དུ་ཡོད་པ་བཞིན་རང་གི་ནང་གི་སེམས་ཀྱི་རང་སྣང་ཙམ་དུ་ཤེས་པར་བྱའོ། །

གཉིས་པ།

གཅིག་ཤོས་ཐུན་མོང་མ་ཡིན་པའི།
གཟུང་བ་རྣམ་པར་རིག་པའི་དོན།
གཞན་གྱི་སེམས་ལ་སོགས་པ་ནི།
མཉམ་པར་མ་གཞག་མཉམ་གཞག་པའི།
འཛིན་པའི་རྣམ་པར་རིག་པ་ལ།
ཕན་ཚུན་ཡུལ་གྱུར་མ་ཡིན་ཏེ།
མཉམ་པར་མ་གཞག་དག་ལ་ནི།
རང་གི་རྣམ་རྟོག་སྣང་ཕྱིར་དང་།
མཉམ་པར་གཞག་པ་དག་ལ་ནི།
ཏིང་འཛིན་དེ་ཡི་སྤྱོད་ཡུལ་དེའི།
གཟུགས་བརྙན་རབ་ཏུ་སྣང་ཕྱིར་རོ།

གང་སྣང་བ་ཐམས་ཅད་སེམས་ལ་སྣང་བ་ཡིན་པ་ཙམ་ནི་སུས་ཀྱང་བཟློག་མི་ནུས་མོད་ཀྱི། དེས་སྣང་བ་ཐམས་ཅད་སེམས་དང་རྫས་གཅིག་ཏུ་སྒྲུབ་པ་དང་། སྣང་བ་གཏོད་བྱེད་ཀྱི་ཕྱི་དོན་མེད་པར་མི་འགྲུབ་སྟེ། ཇི་ལྟར་ན་གཞན་གྱི་སེམས་ཀྱང་གཞན་གྱིས་མངོན་སུམ་

cause for their appearing to be similar will not be the existence of a referent on the outside. Just as something which one type of being sees as water will be seen as existing under another appearance by others among the six types of beings whose karmic impressions differ, anything perceived should be understood to be neither more nor less than a self-manifestation of the mentality internal to a specific observer.

2) The elimination of any further uncertainty

The counterpart is the one in which what is perceived
Is not shared in common. Here awareness' referent
Is the minds and so on associated with others.
These do not comprise an object of mutual exchange
For perceiving awareness not resting nor resting poised,
Because, for those not resting in equipoise,
It is but their own conceptions that appear;
And because, for those who are resting in equipoise,
It is its faithful reflection that appears
As the object encountered during samadhi absorption.

The following objection could be raised: "No one indeed could disprove that all appearances are merely what appears to the mind. This does not, however, prove that all appearances are substantially identical with mind, nor does it prove the non-existence of outer referents producing the appearances, since it is possible for the minds of others to be known directly by

ཞེས་པ་ཡོད་ཀྱང་དེས་ཕྱི་དོན་བཞིན་དུ་རྒྱུད་གཞན་གྱི་སེམས་མེད་པར་སྒྲུབ་པ་དང་། ཕ་རོལ་གྱི་སེམས་སྣང་བ་དེ་རང་གི་སེམས་དང་རྫས་གཅིག་ཏུ་མི་འགྲུབ་པ་བཞིན་ནོ་སྙམ་ན། སྣོད་ཀྱི་འཇིག་རྟེན་སོགས་ཐུན་མོང་པ་ལྟར་སྣང་བ་དེ་ལས་ཅིག་ཤོས་ཐུན་མོང་མ་ཡིན་པའི་གཟུང་བ་གང་ཞིག་རྣམ་པར་རིག་པའམ་ཞེས་པའི་དོན་ནམ་ཡུལ་དུ་གྱུར་པ། སེམས་ཅན་རྒྱུད་གཞན་གྱི་སེམས་དང་སེམས་བྱུང་ལ་སོགས་པ་ཞེས་པ་དེས་ནི། རིགས་སྔགས་དང་བསམ་གཏན་ལ་སོགས་པའི་སྟོབས་ཀྱིས་ཕ་རོལ་གྱི་སེམས་ཇི་ལྟར་གྱུར་པ་ཤེས་སུ་ཟིན་ཀྱང་། ཡུལ་ཅན་མཉམ་པར་མ་གཞག་པ་དང་མཉམ་པར་གཞག་པའི་དུས་ཀྱི་འཛིན་པའི་རྣམ་པར་རིག་པ་ལ་རྒྱུད་ཐ་དད་པའི་སེམས་གཅིག་ལ་གཅིག་ཕན་ཚུན་དངོས་སུ་ཡུལ་དུ་གྱུར་པ་མ་ཡིན་ཏེ། ཇི་ལྟར་ན་མཉམ་པར་མ་གཞག་པ་དག་ལ་ནི། རང་གི་རྣམ་པར་རྟོག་པ་ཕ་རོལ་གྱི་སེམས་དང་འདྲ་བའི་རྣམ་པར་སྣང་བའི་ཕྱིར་དང་། མཉམ་པར་གཞག་པ་དག་ལ་ནི། ཏིང་འཛིན་དེ་ཡི་སྤྱོད་ཡུལ་དུ་འདས་མ་འོངས་མཁྱེན་པའི་རྣམ་པ་དང་འདྲ་བར་ཕ་རོལ་གྱི་སེམས་དེའི་གཟུགས་བརྙན་ཏེ་དེ་དང་འདྲ་བའི་རྣམ་པ་ཙམ་རབ་ཏུ་སྣང་བ་ཡིན་པའི་ཕྱིར་རོ། །

དེས་ན་སེམས་ཡུལ་ལ་དམིགས་ནས་དེའི་རྣམ་པར་སྐྱེ་བ་དང་། སེམས་རང་ཉིད་དང་རྫས་གཅིག་ཏུ་སྨྱོང་བའི་ངོ་བོར་སྐྱེས་པའི་ཡུལ་ཞེས་ཚུལ་གཉིས་མི་འདྲ་སྟེ། རྣལ་འབྱོར་པས། ཕལ་པའི་སེམས་ཀྱི་བདེ་སྡུག་སོགས་དམིགས་པའི་ཚུལ་གྱིས་ཤེས་ཀྱང་། དེ་དང་སྨྱོང་བ་འདྲ་བར་མི་འགྱུར་བ་བཞིན་ནོ། །

someone with extrasensory perception. And this means that there is no validity in saying that the mind appearing to the other person should be substantially identical to the observing mind or that the continuum of that appearing mind does not exist. And the same would apply to outer objects."

To which the reply would be as follows. *The counterpart* to the case of the seemingly shared experience of such things as the world of the vessel *is the one in which* the *referent* or object *perceived is not shared in common.* This refers to the *awareness* or consciousness, i.e., *the minds and* mental states,[23] *associated with other* sentient being*s*.

This *does not comprise an object of mutual exchange* in a direct fashion between the discrete continuum of one mind and that of another, neither *for* the *perceiving awareness* of an observer who is *not resting* in equipoise *nor* for one *resting poised* in meditative balance, even when such knowledge of the mind of another has been gained through the efficacy of mantric science, meditative concentration, or in some other comparable fashion.

Why is that? *Because, for those* who are *not resting in equipoise, it is but their own conceptions that appear* as an image resembling the mind of another; *and because, for those who are resting in equipoise, what appears is a faithful reflection* in the sense of being an accurate resemblance of the other's mind. This reflection is similar to the image through which the past and future is known *as the object encountered during samadhi absorption.*

Because this is so, it must be said that there are two distinct facets involved in awareness of another's mind: one in which the observer focusing attention on the mind of another produces an image of it;[24] and one consisting of the experience accompanying [consciousness of another's mind], an experience which is the specific content of the observer's mind alone. These two processes are comparable to the yogi's consciousness of the happiness or suffering or some other state of an ordinary person's mind through focusing on that, without his experience in that connection being the same as that of the other person.

འོ་ན་ཕ་རོལ་གྱི་སེམས་དེ་བཞིན་དུ་ཕྱི་དོན་ཀུང་དངོས་སུ་མ་མྱོང་བར་རྣམ་པ་ཤར་བས་མྱོང་ན་ཅི་འགལ་སྙམ་ན། ནང་གི་བག་ཆགས་སད་པའི་དབང་གིས་ཤེས་པ་ཉིད་དོན་ལྟར་སྣང་བ་དེ་མེད་ན་ཕྱི་དོན་ཡོད་དུ་ཆུག་ཀུང་མི་སྣང་སྟེ། ཡི་དྭགས་ཀྱིས་ཆུ་དང་ནམ་མཁའ་མཐའ་ཡས་པས་གཟུགས་བཞིན་ནོ། །

ནང་གི་བག་ཆགས་གསལ་བར་སད་ན་ཕྱི་དོན་ཡན་གར་བ་ཡོད་མི་དགོས་ཏེ་ཡི་དྭགས་ལ་རྣག་དང་ནམ་མཁའ་མཐའ་ཡས་པ་ལ་ནམ་མཁའི་སྣང་བ་ཀུན་ཏུ་ཁྱབ་པ་བཞིན་ནོ། །

དེས་ན་སྣང་བ་རྣམས་སེམས་ཀྱི་དབང་གིས་བྱུང་བར་ཟད་དེ། སྣང་བའི་དབང་གིས་སེམས་བྱུང་བ་མ་ཡིན་ནོ། །

དེ་བཞིན་དུ་རྒྱུད་གཞན་ནི་གཞན་གྱི་སེམས་ཀྱི་དབང་གིས་བྱུང་བ་མ་ཡིན་ཏེ། གཅིག་མྱ་ངན་ལས་འདས་ཀུང་ཐམས་ཅད་དེ་བཞིན་དུ་འགྱུར་བར་ཁས་ལེན་མི་ནུས་པའི་ཕྱིར་རོ། །

འོ་ན་སངས་རྒྱས་ལ་ཆོས་ཐམས་ཅད་མངོན་སུམ་དུ་གྱུར་བའི་ཕྱིར་དེ་ལ་ཅི་སྣང་བ་དེའི་ཡེ་ཤེས་དང་རྫས་གཅིག་ན་སངས་རྒྱས་དང་སེམས་ཅན་གྱི་ཤེས་རྒྱུད་གཅིག་ཏུ་འགྱུར་རོ་ཞེ་ན། སངས་རྒྱས་ལ་བདག་དང་སེམས་ཅན་ཐ་དད་པའི་རྒྱུད་ཀྱི་འདུ་ཤེས་མི་མངའ་སྟེ་ཆོས་ཉིད་བཞིན་དུ་གནས་ཡོངས་སུ་གྱུར་པའི་ཡེ་ཤེས་ཡིན་པས་ན་དེ་དང་ཆོས་ཐམས་ཅད

The objection could then be raised: "What would be the problem in thinking, 'Well, then, the minds of others exist[25] but are experienced, not directly, but through the medium of an image, and the same would apply to outer objects?'"

In reply, if it were not the case that it is the consciousness itself appearing as an object due to the wakening of internal residual patterns, even granted that outer referents existed, they would not appear, comparable to the case of water for hungry ghosts and forms for the gods of infinite space. If, on the contrary, it were a case of internal residual tendencies manifesting explicitly, outer referents existing on their own would not be needed, comparable to the case of pus for hungry ghosts and the appearance of space literally everywhere for a god of infinite space.

Hence it is evident that it is appearance that manifests through the power of mind, not mind through the power of appearances. Similarly, all others' mindstreams could not be the product of any one mind, since it is not possible to claim that, when *one* has achieved nirvana, all would have done so.

But the objection could be raised: "Because all phenomena are directly manifest for a buddha, whatever appears to him is of the same substance as his wisdom; and since that is the case, would there not be one and the same stream of consciousness for buddhas and sentient beings?"

In reply, buddhas do not entertain notions of their own and sentient beings' mindstreams as being the same or different. Since their wisdom is bound up with a complete transformation in harmony with pure being, it is taught that it cannot be measured in terms of its being the same as or

གཅིག་པ་དང་ཐ་དད་པ་ལ་སོགས་པའི་ཚུལ་དུ་དཔག་པར་མི་ནུས་པར་གསུངས་ཏེ།

མ་སྐྱེས་པ་དང་མི་འགག་པ།
ཆོས་ཉིད་མྱ་ངན་འདས་དང་མཚུངས།

ཞེས་གསུངས་པ་བཞིན་ནོ། །

གཉིས་པ་ནི།

གཟུང་བར་སྣང་བ་མེད་གྲུབ་ན།
འཛིན་པར་སྣང་བ་མེད་གྲུབ་བོ།
དེ་ལས་ཀྱང་ནི་གཟུང་བ་དང་།
འཛིན་པར་སྣང་བ་མེད་པ་ལ།
འཇུག་པ་གྲུབ་སྟེ་ཐོག་མེད་པའི།
ཀུན་ནས་ལྡང་བ་གྲུབ་པས་སོ།
གཉིས་སུ་ཡོངས་སུ་མ་གྲུབ་པར།
རབ་ཏུ་གྲུབ་པ་ཡིན་ཕྱིར་རོ།

དེ་ལྟར་གཟུང་བར་སྣང་བ་དེ་ནི་རང་གི་ངོ་བོས་འཛིན་པ་ལས་གཞན་དུ་མེད་པར་གྲུབ་ན། འཛིན་པར་སྣང་བ་དེ་ཡང་མེད་པར་གྲུབ་བོ། །

དེ་ཅིའི་ཕྱིར་ན་འཛིན་པ་ནི་གཟུང་བ་ལ་ལྟོས་ཏེ་གྲུབ་ཀྱི་ཡན་གར་དུ་ནམ་ཡང་མི་འགྲུབ་བོ། །

different from phenomena, as implied by the following quotation:

> Pure being, equivalent to nirvana,
> Does not involve arising or cessation.

(B) The resultant procedure for approaching reality, the freedom from perceived and perceiver

> *If what appears as perceived does not exist,*
> *Whatever appears as perceiver does not exist;*
> *Due to this, there is also a rationale*
> *Behind the breakthrough to freedom from this appearance*
> *Of perceived and perceiver, because without beginning*
> *A volatile state prevails; and because duality's*
> *Not existing at all is what really exists.*

If what appears as perceived does not exist with an essence of its own distinct from the perceiver, as described above, *whatever appears as perceiver does not exist* either. This is because perceiver exists relative to perceived but never exists on its own.

དེ་ལྟར་ན་གཟུང་བ་དང་འཛིན་པ་གཉིས་ཀྱི་རྣམ་པ་ཐམས་ཅད་དང་བྲལ་ཏེ་ཡུལ་དང་ཡུལ་ཅན་མེད་པའི་རིག་པ་རང་བཞིན་གྱིས་འོད་གསལ་བ་བརྗོད་དུ་མེད་པ་ཙམ་ནི་བདག་གཉིས་ཀྱིས་སྟོང་པའི་ཡོངས་གྲུབ་དེ་བཞིན་ཉིད་དང་ཐ་མི་དད་པ་དེ་ནི་སེམས་ཙམ་པས་ཀྱང་རྟོགས་དགོས་ན་དབུ་མ་པས་ལྟ་ཅི་སྨོས་སོ། །

སེམས་ཙམ་པ་ལྟར་ན་དེའི་རང་བཞིན་ལ་སྟོང་ཉིད་བཅུ་དྲུག་གི་དོན་ཡོངས་སུ་རྫོགས་ཏེ་ཕྱི་དང་ནང་ལ་སོགས་པ་གཟུང་འཛིན་གྱི་ཆོས་གང་དུ་ཡང་བསམ་པ་དང་བརྗོད་པར་བྱ་བ་མ་ཡིན་པས་སྤྲོས་བྲལ་དུ་འདོད་དོ། །

འོན་ཀྱང་བརྗོད་མེད་ཀྱི་ཤེས་པ་དེ་ཡི་ངོ་བོ་ལ་བདེན་གྲུབ་ཏུ་འཛོག་ཚུལ་གྱི་གྲུབ་མཐའ་ཕྲ་མོ་ཙམ་ཞིག་ལྷག་མར་ལུས་པ་དེ་ཉིད་རིགས་པས་སུན་ཕྱུང་སྟེ་གཟུང་འཛིན་མེད་པའི་ཤེས་པ་ཉིད་ཀྱང་བདེན་པ་མེད་པའི་སྟོང་པ་དང་ཟུང་དུ་ཞུགས་པའི་རང་སེམས་གདོད་ནས་དག་པའི་འོད་གསལ་ཉིད་དུ་འདོད་ན་དབུ་མ་ཡང་དག་པ་ཡིན་ཏེ། དེས་ན་ཐེག་ཆེན་དབུ་སེམས་འདི་གཉིས་ཞེན་པའི་གནད་ཕྲ་མོ་ཞིག་ཚོད་མ་ཚོད་ཀྱི་ཁྱད་པར་ལས། མཉམ་རྗེས་ཀྱི་ཉམས་ལེན་ཕྱོགས་འདྲ་བ་ལྟ་བུར་འོང་བས་འཕགས་ཡུལ་གྱི་པཎ་གྲུབ་ཆེན་པོ་རྣམས་ཀྱང་ཐེག་པ་ཆེན་པོ་ཉམས་སུ་ལེན་པ་ལ་འདི་གཉིས་ཁྱད་མེད་ལྟ་བུར་མཛད་པའང་དོན་དེ་ལྟ་བུའི་ཕྱིར་ཡིན་ནོ། །

This being the case, the awareness not involving an object/observer relation in being free of all aspects of perceived-perceiver duality is by nature ineffable clear light itself. It is not differentiable from suchness, the actually present aspect empty of the two forms of self-entity. If it is this which even a practitioner of the Chittamatra must realize, what need to mention a practitioner of the Madhyamaka?

According to the Chittamatra, all sixteen types of emptiness[26] are fully included within this nature. It cannot be conceived or formulated in terms of "outer," "inner," or any other phenomenon associated with perceived and perceiver, and is therefore asserted to be free of conceptual elaborations.

Nevertheless, a slight remnant of a subtle hypothetical tenet persists within the Chittamatra system in the sense that true existence is posited for the essence of this ineffable consciousness. If one demonstrates the flaws in this supposition through logical reasoning and asserts that this consciousness itself, which is free of perceived and perceiver, is also devoid of true existence, such that mind itself is a union of this emptiness and primordially pure clear light, this is authentic Madhyamaka.

A distinction can, therefore, be made between these two Mahayana schools, Chittamatra and Madhyamaka, with respect to the crucial point of whether this subtle assumption has been cut through or not, but the meditative and post meditative phases as practiced in both are so nearly identical that even the great pandits and mahasiddhas of the noble land (India) with good reason made no distinction between the two as far as the actual practice of Mahayana is concerned.

གོང་དུ་བཤད་པ་གཟུང་འཛིན་གཉིས་མེད་པའི་ཚུལ་ཤེས་པ་དེ་ལས་ཀྱང་ནི་དེ་ཡི་དོན་ལ་རྩེ་གཅིག་ཏུ་མཉམ་པར་བཞག་པ་ལས་གཟུང་བ་དང་འཛིན་པར་སྣང་བ་མེད་པ་ལ་མངོན་སུམ་དུ་འཇུག་པ་གྲུབ་སྟེ་གཉིས་སུ་མེད་པའི་ཆོས་ཉིད་མཐོང་བར་འགྱུར་རོ། །

གཉིས་སུ་མེད་པའི་ཆོས་ཉིད་དེ་ལྟ་བུ་ཡེ་ནས་ཡོངས་སུ་གྲུབ་པའམ། ཡོད་བཞིན་དུ་དེ་མི་སྣང་བར་གཉིས་སུ་སྣང་བའི་འཁྲུལ་པ་དེ་འབྱུང་བར་མི་འཐད་སྙམ་ན། དེ་ལ་མི་འཐད་པ་མེད་དེ་ཐོག་མ་མེད་པའི་དུས་ནས་བརྒྱུད་དེ་འོངས་པའི་གཟུང་འཛིན་གཉིས་སྣང་གི་བག་ཆགས་གང་ཞིག་དེ་ཁོ་ན་ཉིད་ལ་སྒྲིབ་པར་བྱེད་པའི་ཚུལ་ཅན་སེམས་ཀྱི་རང་བཞིན་འོད་གསལ་བ་དང་ལྷན་ཅིག་གནས་པ་དེ་ཉིད་ཀུན་ནས་ལྡང་བའམ་མངོན་དུ་སད་པའམ་རྣམ་པར་སྨིན་པ་ཉིད་དུ་གྱུར་པས་ན། རྒྱུ་དེ་ལས་འཁྲུལ་ཞིང་འཁོར་བ་འབྱུང་བ་ཡིན་ཞེས་སོ། །

འོ་ན་ཐོག་མ་མེད་པ་ནས་ལྷན་སྐྱེས་སུ་གནས་པའི་ཕྱིར་དེ་ཡང་སྤང་མི་ནུས་སམ་སྙམ་ན། དེ་མ་ཡིན་ཏེ་གཟུང་འཛིན་གཉིས་ཡོངས་སུ་མ་གྲུབ་པར་རབ་ཏུ་གྲུབ་པ་ཡིན་པའི་ཕྱིར་དེ་ལྟར་རྟོགས་ནས་བསྒོམ་པ་ན་དེ་མངོན་དུ་མཐོང་བར་འགྱུར་རོ་ཞེས་གཉིས་མེད་ལ་འཇུག་པ་གྲུབ་པའི་འཐད་པ་བརྗོད་པ་ཡིན་ནོ། །

Due to this knowledge of the way freedom from perceived and perceiver is explained above, *there is also a rationale behind the* direct *breakthrough to freedom from this appearance of perceived and perceiver* in which pure being free of duality is seen by resting one-pointedly in its reality during meditative equipoise.

One might consider it untenable for non-dual pure being to actually be present—i.e., to exist—from the outset yet not appear, while dualistic appearances, which are a delusion, manifest. But this is not untenable *because*, throughout the course of time *without beginning*, the habitual tendency toward appearance involving perceived-perceiver dualism coexists with the clear light nature of mind in a manner which obscures that very nature, such that *a volatile state*, that is, an excitable condition or state of ferment, *prevails*, thus providing the cause through which delusion originates hand in hand with samsara.

Then again, one might suppose that, as a consequence of their coexisting in a beginningless fashion, dualistic appearance would be impossible to relinquish, but this is not the case either, *because* the *duality* of perceived and perceiver's *not existing at all is what really exists.* When one meditates with such an understanding, this will be seen directly.

This completes the formulation of the reasoning providing the rationale behind the breakthrough to freedom from duality.

གཉིས་པ་ཆོས་ཉིད་རྒྱས་པར་བཤད་པ་ལ། སྡོམ་གྱིས་མདོར་བསྟན་པ་དང་། སྡོམ་དོན་རྒྱས་པར་བཤད་པ་གཉིས། །དང་པོ།

རྣམ་པ་དྲུག་གིས་ཆོས་ཉིད་ལ།
འཇུག་པ་བླ་ན་མེད་པ་སྟེ།
མཚན་ཉིད་ཀུན་ཏུ་གནས་པ་དང་།
ངེས་པར་འབྱེད་དང་རེག་པ་དང་།
རྗེས་སུ་དྲན་དང་དེའི་བདག་ཉིད།
ཉེ་བར་སོན་ལ་འཇུག་པས་སོ།

དོན་རྣམ་པ་དྲུག་གིས་ཆོས་ཉིད་ལ་འཇུག་པ་བླ་ན་མེད་པ་སྟེ། གང་ཞིག་དོན་དྲུག་པོ་དེ་ཁོང་དུ་ཆུད་ན་རྣམ་བྱང་གི་ཆོས་མ་ལུས་པ་བདེ་བླག་ཏུ་ཁོང་དུ་ཆུད་པར་འགྱུར་བའི་ཕྱིར་རོ། །དེ་གང་ཞེ་ན། ཆོས་ཉིད་ཀྱི་མཚན་ཉིད་ཤེས་པར་བྱ་བ་དང་། དེ་སྐྱེ་བའི་གནས་སམ་གཞི་ཉིད་དུ་གྱུར་པའོ། །ཡང་ན་ཆོས་ཉིད་དེ་དམིགས་པ་གང་ལ་ཀུན་ཏུ་གནས་པ་དེའི་གཞི་དང་། དེ་ངེས་པར་འབྱེད་དང་། ཆོས་ཉིད་ཀྱི་དོན་ལ་མངོན་སུམ་རེག་པ་དང་། སླར་ཡང་དེ་ཉིད་ཡང་ནས་ཡང་དུ་རྗེས་སུ་དྲན་པ་དང་། ཆོས་ཉིད་དེའི་བདག་ཉིད་དུ་ཉེ་བར་སོན་པའམ་ཡོངས་སུ་གྲུབ་པ་མཐར་ཕྱིན་པ་ལ་འཇུག་པ་དང་དྲུག་གིས་སོ། །

II) The expanded explanation of pure being

A) A brief presentation of the headings
B) The expanded explanation of these six

A) A brief presentation of the headings

Through introducing traits and a ground at all times,
Definitive verification as well as encounter,
Recollection and immersion into its core,
This sixpoint approach to pure being is unsurpassed.

This six-point approach to pure being is unsurpassed, since anyone who has understood these six points will easily comprehend all qualities without exception related to the process of refinement.

And how does this approach lead to such a result? It does so *through introducing* [the student to the first of the six points, namely] the knowledge of the defining *traits* of pure being as well as to [the last five,] which constitute the sole ground or basis for gaining access to such traits.

To look more closely [at the last five, they consist of:] that focus with respect to which there is *a ground* or basis for pure being *at all times;* the *definitive verification* of pure being itself, *as well as* the direct *encounter* with it; *the* renewed *recollection* of precisely this again and again; and *immersion into its* very *core,* meaning the final breakthrough to that nature which is actually present.

གཉིས་པ་སྦྱོར་གྱི་དོན་བཞིན་དྲུག་པོ་དེ་སོ་སོར་བཤད་པ་ལ། དང་པོ།

མཚན་ཉིད་མདོ་ནི་ཇི་ལྟ་བཞིན།

ཆོས་ཉིད་རྣམ་བྱང་གི་མཚན་ཉིད་གང་ཞེ་ན་གོང་དུ་མདོ་རུ་བསྡུས་ཏེ་བསྟན་པའི་སྐབས་སུ་དེ་བཞིན་ཉིད་གཟུང་བ་སོགས་བཞི་དང་བྲལ་བར་ནི་བསྟན་པ་ཇི་ལྟ་བར་ཤེས་པར་བྱའོ། །

གཉིས་པ།

གནས་ནི་ཆོས་རྣམས་ཐམས་ཅད་དང་།

གསུང་རབ་མདོ་སྡེ་ཐམས་ཅད་དོ།

གནས་ནི་བརྗོད་བྱ་ཀུན་བྱང་གིས་བསྡུས་པའི་ཤེས་བྱའི་ཆོས་རྣམས་ཐམས་ཅད་དང་། རྗོད་བྱེད་གསུང་རབ་ཡན་ལག་བཅུ་གཉིས་ཀྱིས་བསྡུས་པའི་མདོ་སྡེ་ཐམས་ཅད་ཡིན་པར་འདོད་དོ། །

ཅིའི་ཕྱིར་ཞེ་ན། ཆོས་ཐམས་ཅད་ལ་ཐ་སྙད་དུ་བླང་དོར་ལ་སོགས་པའི་ཚུལ་དང་དོན་དམ་པར་མི་དམིགས་པར་གཏན་ལ་ཕབ་པ་ལས་མྱང་འདས་ཐོབ་པ་དང་། གསུང་རབ་ལ་ཐོས་བསམ་གྱིས་ཞུགས་པ་ལས་ལམ་སྒྲུབ་ཚུལ་ལ་མ་རྨོངས་པར་འགྱུར་བའི་ཕྱིར་རོ། །

B) The expanded explanation of these six

(1) The defining characteristics

The defining traits in brief are just as they are.

If one is seeking to know *the defining traits* of pure being, the state of complete refinement, one should know that they *are just as these are* described *in* the *brief* summary above, where the suchness is taught as being free of four factors, a perceived and so on.

(2) The ground

The ground consists of the whole of phenomena
And supreme teachings, the whole of the sutra collections.

The ground is asserted to *consist of* the subject taught and its formulation.[27] The subject taught is *the whole of phenomena,* meaning all objects of knowledge comprising affliction and refinement; its formulation is found in *the whole of the sutra collections,* which consist of the twelve branches of the *supreme teachings.*

The reason [the term "ground" is applied to the first of these] is that nirvana is attained, in a conventional sense, through such means as the adoption or rejection relevant to any phenomenon and, in genuine reality, through gaining a firm understanding of there being no phenomena on which to focus.

[The term "ground" is applied to the second] because freedom from unclarity about how to practice the path is gained through the pursuit of listening to and reflecting over the supreme teachings.

གསུམ་པ།

དེ་ལ་ངེས་པར་འབྱེད་པ་ནི།
ཐེག་པ་ཆེན་པོའི་མདོ་སྡེ་ལ།
བརྟེན་པའི་ཚུལ་བཞིན་ཡིད་བྱེད་པས།
བསྡུས་པའི་སྦྱོར་ལམ་ཐམས་ཅད་དོ།

དོན་དེ་ལ་ངེས་པར་འབྱེད་པ་ཞེས་བྱ་བ་ནི། ཐེག་པ་ཆེན་པོའི་མདོ་སྡེ་ཡི་དགོངས་དོན་ལ་བརྟེན་པའི་ཚུལ་བཞིན་ཡིད་ལ་བྱེད་པས་བསྡུས་པའི་སྦྱོར་ལམ་ཐམས་ཅད་ལ་བཤད་དོ། །ཅིའི་ཕྱིར་ངེས་འབྱེད་ཅེས་བྱ་སྙམ་ན། ཚོགས་སྦྱོར་དུ་མདོ་སྡེའི་དོན་བཞིན་ཤེས་རབ་གསུམ་གྱི་སྒོ་ནས་ཡིད་ལ་བྱས་པས་ཆོས་ཉིད་ཀྱི་དོན་ངེས་པར་འབྱེད་པའམ་ངོས་ཟིན་པ་ལ་དེ་སྐད་དུ་བྱས་སོ། །

བཞི་པ།

རིག་པ་ཡང་དག་ལྟ་ཐོབ་ཕྱིར།
མཐོང་བའི་ལམ་གྱིས་མངོན་སུམ་གྱི།
ཚུལ་དུ་དེ་བཞིན་ཉིད་ཐོབ་ཅིང་།
ཉམས་སུ་མྱོང་བ་གང་ཡིན་པའོ།

རིག་པ་ཞེས་བྱ་བ་ནི་ཡུལ་ཅན་ཤེས་རབ་ཀྱི་སྤྱན་ནས་འཇིག་རྟེན་ལས་འདས་པའི་ཡང་དག་པའི་ལྟ་བ་ཐོབ་པའི་ཕྱིར་མཐོང་བའི་ལམ་གྱིས་དོན་སྤྱི་ཙམ་མ་ཡིན་པར་མཉམ་བཞག་ཏུ་མངོན་སུམ་གྱི་ཚུལ་དུ་ཡུལ་དེ་བཞིན་ཉིད་མཐོང་སྣང་གི་དྲི་མས་དག་པ་མངོན་དུ་ཐོབ་ཅིང་། རྗེས་ཐོབ་ཏུ་ཡང་དག་པའི་ལྟ་བས་ཉམས་སུ་མྱོང་བ་གང་ཡིན་པའོ། །

(3) Definitive verification

> *The term "definitive verification of this"*
> *Refers to the whole of the path of application,*
> *Composed of appropriate mental cultivation*
> *Based on the sutra collections of Mahayana.*

The term "definitive verification of the meaning of *this"* is explained as *referring to the whole of the path of application,* which *is composed of appropriate mental cultivation based on* the intended meaning of *the sutra collections of Mahayana.*

If one wonders why the term "definitive verification" is used, it indicates that, through cultivating the mind on the paths of accumulation and application by nurturing the three types of precise knowledge in accord with the content of the sutra collections, the meaning of pure being is definitively verified, that is to say, confirmed.

(4) Encounter

> *The encounter attained because of authentic view*
> *Is the path of vision, on which the suchness attained*
> *Is in a fashion direct, whatever experienced.*

The fourth point is called "*encounter,*" *because authentic view* which transcends the world has here been *attained* with the eye of knowledge as the seer. This *is the path of vision on which the* object, *suchness*—purged of all defilements eliminated through seeing—is actually *attained* during meditative equipoise *in a fashion* which *is* wholly *direct,* not merely as an abstract idea. *Whatever* is *experienced* during the post- meditative state is then seen from the perspective of authentic view.

ལྔ་པ།

རྗེས་སུ་དྲན་པ་རིག་པས་ནི།
མཐོང་བའི་དོན་ལ་སྒོམ་ལམ་གྱི།
བྱང་ཆུབ་ཕྱོགས་ཀྱིས་བསྡུས་པ་སྟེ།
དེ་ནི་དྲི་མ་སེལ་བའི་ཕྱིར།

རྗེས་སུ་དྲན་པ་ཞེས་བྱ་བ་ནི་སྔར་སོ་སོ་རང་རིག་པས་ནི་ཆོས་ཉིད་མངོན་སུམ་མཐོང་བའི་དོན་རྟོགས་ཟིན་ལ། སླར་ཡང་བསྒོམ་པའི་ལམ་གྱི་སྐབས་ན་ཡང་ཡང་དྲན་ཞིང་རྟོགས་པར་བྱེད་པ་བྱང་ཆུབ་ཀྱི་ཕྱོགས་ཀྱིས་བསྡུས་པ་ཐམས་ཅད་ལ་དེ་ལྟར་བརྗོད་པ་སྟེ། བསྒོམ་ལམ་དེ་ནི་བསྒོམ་པས་སྤང་བར་བྱ་བའི་དྲི་མ་རྣམས་སེལ་བའི་ཕྱིར་བསྒོམ་པའོ། །

(5) Recollection

Although reality ***has*** *been seen by awareness,*
Recollection—the path of meditation,
Composed of factors inducing enlightenment—
Is needed to eliminate the stains.

Although reality—pure being—*has* already *been seen* directly and realized *by* intimate, detailed self-*awareness* on the previous stage, what is here referred to as "*recollection*" *is composed of* all those *factors inducing enlightenment* that enable one to recollect and realize this again and again throughout a process of repeated habituation.[28] This is *the path of meditation*, where one practices in order *to eliminate* all those *stains* which only meditation can remove.

དྲུག་པ་ལ་མཐར་ཐུག་གི་གནས་ཡོངས་སུ་གྱུར་པའི་ངོ་བོ་ངོས་བཟུང་བ་དང་། དེའི་ཁྱད་པར་གྱི་ཆོས་རྣམས་རྒྱས་པར་བཤད་པ་གཉིས། དང་པོ།

དེ་ལ་དེ་ཡི་བདག་ཉིད་དུ།
ཉེ་བར་སྟོན་པ་དེ་བཞིན་ཉིད།
དྲི་མ་མེད་པར་གྱུར་པ་ན།
ཐམས་ཅད་དེ་བཞིན་ཉིད་ཙམ་དུ།
སྣང་བ་དེ་ཡང་གནས་གྱུར་པ།
གྲུབ་པ་ཡིན་ནོ'''

དང་པོ་ཆོས་ཐམས་ཅད་ཀྱི་གནས་ལུགས་དེ་བཞིན་ཉིད་དེ་ལ་དེ་ཡི་བདག་ཉིད་དུ་ཉེ་བར་སྟོན་པ་ནི་དེ་བཞིན་ཉིད་དེ་གློ་བུར་གྱི་དྲི་མ་མེད་པ་གྱུར་པ་ན། གནས་སྣང་རྣམ་པ་ཀུན་ཏུ་མཚུངས་པར་གྱུར་ཏེ་ཆོས་ཐམས་ཅད་དེ་བཞིན་ཉིད་ཙམ་དུ་སྣང་བ་ཡིན་ལ། དེ་ཡང་དེའི་ཚེ་གནས་གྱུར་པ་ཡོངས་སུ་རྫོགས་པ་ཉིད་དུ་གྲུབ་པ་ཡིན་ནོ། །ཞེས་གནས་གྱུར་ཙམ་ས་དང་པོ་ནས་ཡོད་ཀྱང་མཐར་ཐུག་གི་ས་འདིར་གནས་གྱུར་མཐར་ཐུག་གྲུབ་པ་ཡིན་ནོ། །ཞེས་སོ། །

(6) Complete immersion into its core

(I) The character of ultimate transformation

(II) The expanded explanation of its distinctive features

(I) The character of ultimate transformation

Here, immersion into its core complete,
Is suchness rendered free of any stain,
Where all appear exclusively as suchness—
And this completes the transformation as well.

Here is the point at which *immersion into the core* of that suchness which is the abiding nature of all phenomena has been *complete*d. This *is* the *suchness rendered free of any* superficial *stain, where all* phenomena—whose fundamental being and appearance have been reconciled in every respect—*appear exclusively as suchness. And this completes the transformation* in its fullest sense *as well.*

Transformation as such is present from the first bodhisattva level onwards, but it is at this final level that ultimate transformation is accomplished.

གཉིས་པ་ལ་མདོར་བསྟན་པ་དང་རྒྱས་པར་བཤད་པ་གཉིས། དང་པོ།

'''རྣམ་པ་བཅུས།

གནས་ཡོངས་གྱུར་ལ་འཇུག་པ་ནི།
བླ་ན་མེད་པ་ཉིད་ཡིན་ཏེ།
ངོ་བོ་རྫས་དང་གང་ཟག་དང་།
ཁྱད་པར་དགོས་པ་གནས་དང་ནི།
ཡིད་ལ་བྱེད་དང་སྦྱོར་བ་དང་།
ཉེས་དམིགས་ཕན་ཡོན་འཇུག་པས་སོ།

དོན་རྣམ་པ་བཅུས་གནས་ཡོངས་སུ་གྱུར་པ་ལ་ཤེས་ཤིང་སྒྲུབ་པའི་ཚུལ་གྱིས་འཇུག་པ་ནི། བླ་ན་མེད་པ་ཉིད་ཡིན་ཏེ་བཅུ་པོ་དེས་གནས་ཡོངས་སུ་གྱུར་པའི་དོན་ཇི་ལྟ་བ་བཞིན་དུ་ཁོང་དུ་ཆུད་ཅིང་དེ་སྒྲུབ་པ་ལས་འབྲས་བུའི་མཐར་ཐུག་ཐོབ་པའི་ཕྱིར་རོ། །

བཅུ་པོ་དེ་གང་ཞེ་ན། རང་བཞིན་ནམ་ངོ་བོ་དང་། དངོས་པོའམ་རྫས་དང་། གང་ཟག་དང་། ཁྱད་པར་དང་། དགོས་པ་དང་། དེའི་གནས་སམ་རྟེན་གང་ཡིན་པ་དང་ནི། ཡིད་ལ་བྱེད་པ་དང་། སྦྱོར་བ་དང་། དེ་མེད་པའི་ཉེས་དམིགས་དང་། ཡོད་པའི་ཕན་ཡོན་ལ་འཇུག་པས་སོ། །

(II) The expanded explanation of its distinctive features

(A) The brief presentation of the headings
(B) The expansion on these ten

(A) The brief presentation of the headings

This ten-point presentation of transformation
Provides an unsurpassable introduction,
Because it is the way to approach the essence,
The ingredients and individuals,
The special traits, requirements, and ground,
Mental cultivation and application,
The disadvantages and benefits.

This ten-point presentation enabling knowledge as well as accomplishment *of* thorough *transformation provides an unsurpassable introduction, because it is the way* one comprehends what is actually meant by thorough transformation and puts it into practice, thereby attaining the ultimate among results.

To name the ten which make up this *approach*, they include *the essence* or nature of the transformation, its *ingredients* or contents as well as the *individuals* who are transformed, its *special traits* and *requirements and* what constitutes its *ground* or support, its *mental cultivation and application,* as well as *the disadvantages* that would follow if there were no such thing as this transformation *and* the *benefits* that follow because there is.

གཉིས་པ་མདོར་བསྟན་གྱི་རིམ་པ་དང་མཚུངས་པར་རྒྱས་བཤད་བཅུ་ལས། དང་པོ།

དེ་ལ་ངོ་བོར་འཇུག་པ་ནི།
གློ་བུར་བ་ཡི་དྲི་མ་དང་།
དེ་བཞིན་ཉིད་མི་སྣང་བ་དང་།
སྣང་བའི་དོན་དུ་དེ་བཞིན་ཉིད།
དྲི་མ་མེད་པ་གང་ཡིན་པའོ།

དེ་ལ་རང་བཞིན་ནམ་ངོ་བོར་འཇུག་པ་ནི། གློ་བུར་བ་ཡི་དྲི་མ་དང་། དེ་བཞིན་ཉིད་རིམ་པ་བཞིན་མི་སྣང་བ་དང་སྣང་བའི་དོན་དུ་ཆོས་ཉིད་དེ་བཞིན་ཉིད་དེ་གློ་བུར་གྱི་དྲི་མ་མེད་པ་གང་ཡིན་པ་སྟེ་ཆོས་ཉིད་དྲི་བྲལ་རང་གི་ངོ་བོ་ཇི་བཞིན་པར་སྣང་བའོ། །

(B) The expansion on these ten

1) The essence

> *The essence of transformation is introduced*
> *As suchness freed of stain, and what that means*
> *Is superficial stains appear no longer*
> *And that which manifests is now the suchness.*

The essence—i.e., makeup—*of transformation is introduced as* consisting of the *suchness*—pure being—*freed of* superficial *stain. That means, superficial stains appear no longer and suchness manifests*; that is to say, pure being, which is free of stain in its very essence, manifests just as it is.[29]

གཉིས་པ།

> དངོས་པོ་རྫས་ལ་འཇུག་པ་ནི།
> ཐུན་མོང་སྣོད་ཀྱི་རྣམ་རིག་པ།
> དེ་བཞིན་ཉིད་དུ་གྱུར་པ་དང་།
> མདོ་སྡེ་ཆོས་ཀྱི་དབྱིངས་ཉིད་ཀྱི།
> དེ་བཞིན་ཉིད་དུ་གྱུར་པ་དང་།
> ཐུན་མོང་མིན་པ་སེམས་ཅན་གྱི།
> ཁམས་ཀྱི་རྣམ་པར་རིག་པ་ཡི།
> དེ་བཞིན་ཉིད་དུ་གྱུར་པའོ།

གནས་ཡོངས་སུ་གྱུར་པ་དེའི་དངོས་པོའམ་རྫས་ཉིད་ལ་འཇུག་པ་ནི་སྐབས་འདིར་རྣམ་པ་གསུམ་དུ་བསྡུསཏེ་བསྟན་པ་ནི་ཐུན་མོང་བ་ལྟར་སྣང་བ་སྣོད་ཀྱི་འཇིག་རྟེན་གྱི་རྣམ་པར་རིག་པའམ་རྣམ་པར་སྣང་བ་དེ་བཞིན་ཉིད་དུ་གནས་ཡོངས་སུ་གྱུར་པ་དང་། མིང་ཚིག་ཡི་གེའི་རྣམ་པར་སྣང་བའི་རྗོད་བྱེད་དུ་གྱུར་པ་མདོ་སྡེ་རྣམས་ཀྱི་ཆོས་ཀྱི་དབྱིངས་ཉིད་ཀྱི་དེ་བཞིན་ཉིད་དུ་གྱུར་པ་དང་། ཐུན་མོང་མིན་པ་རྒྱུད་སོ་སོར་བསྡུས་པའི་སེམས་ཅན་གྱི་ཁམས་ཀྱི་སེམས་སེམས་བྱུང་གི་རྣམ་པར་རིག་པ་ཡི་ཚོགས་དེ་བཞིན་ཉིད་དུ་གནས་གྱུར་པ་དང་གསུམ་གྱི་ཚུལ་དུ་ཤེས་པར་བྱའོ། །

2) The ingredients

To introduce the ingredients, or contents:
Awareness in the form of the vessel shared
Undergoes a transformation to suchness;
The sutras undergo a transformation
Into the suchness, the actual dharmadhatu;
And beings' awareness-components not shared in common
Undergo a transformation to suchness.

To introduce the ingredients, that is, the *contents* of this complete transformation, this subject is here summarized under three points.

Image-*awareness,* meaning that which appears *in the form of the* world of the *vessel,* which is seemingly *shared* in common, *undergoes a* complete *transformation to suchness.*

The signifiers appearing in the form of the letters, terms, and statements *of the sutra* texts and the dharmadhatu they teach *undergo a* complete *transformation into the suchness,* which is *the actual dharmadhatu.*

And the principles of *awareness,* consisting of conscious mind and mental states, which are the *components of beings* that comprise their individual mindstreams and are *not shared in common,* also *undergo a transformation to suchness.* One should know the transformation takes these three forms.

དེ་ལ་ཆོས་ཀྱི་དབྱིངས་ལས་མ་གཏོགས་པའི་ཆོས་འགའ་ཙམ་ཡང་ཡོད་པ་མ་ཡིན་པས་ན་གནས་གྱུར་པའི་ཚེ་ཟག་པ་མེད་པའི་དབྱིངས་ན་ཆོས་ཅན་རྣམ་པ་ཐམས་ཅད་པའི་མཐའ་དང་མཉམ་པའི་གནས་གྱུར་གྱི་ཡོན་ཏན་བསམ་གྱིས་མི་ཁྱབ་པ་ཡོད་ཀྱང་། འདིར་སྣོད་དང་དེའི་ཤུགས་ཀྱིས་ལུས་སུ་སྣང་བ་ཐམས་ཅད་གནས་གྱུར་བའི་མཐའ་དབུས་མེད་པའི་དེ་བཞིན་ཉིད་བརྡལ་བ་ཆོས་སྐུ་ཐོབ་པ་དང་། གཉིས་པ་མདོ་སྡེས་མཚོན་པའི་ངག་གི་འདུ་བྱེད་དུ་གཏོགས་པ་ཐམས་ཅད་གནས་གྱུར་པའི་ཆོས་ཀྱི་སྒྲ་དབྱངས་རྒྱུན་ཆད་པ་མེད་ཅིང་ཟད་མི་ཤེས་པའི་ཡོན་ཏན་ལ་དབང་འབྱོར་པ་ལོངས་སྐུ་ཐོབ་པ་དང་། སེམས་ཀྱིས་བསྡུས་པ་ཀུན་གཞི་དང་དེ་ལ་བརྟེན་པའི་ཚོགས་བདུན་གནས་གྱུར་པ་ཡེ་ཤེས་ལྔའི་མཁྱེན་པ་དང་ལྡན་པ་སྤྲུལ་པའི་སྐུ་ཐོབ་པའོ། །

ཡང་ན་རིམ་པ་བཞིན་ཞིང་དང་ལུས་ཡོངས་སུ་དག་པར་སྣང་བ་དང་། དམ་པའི་ཆོས་འདོམས་པ་དང་། ཇི་ལྟ་ཇི་སྙེད་ཀྱི་ཡེ་ཤེས་ཀྱིས་ཤེས་བྱའི་རྣམ་པ་ཐམས་ཅད་ལུང་སྟོན་པའི་ཁྱད་པར་དུ་བལྟ་བར་བྱའོ། །

དེ་ལ་གཟུགས་ཅན་དང་ངག་གི་སྒྲར་བསྡུས་པ་ནི་གནས་མ་གྱུར་པའི་སྐབས་ན་ཕྱིན་མོང་དུ་སྣང་རུང་བ། སེམས་ནི་ཐུན་མོང་མིན་པ་ཡིན་ལ། གནས་གྱུར་པའི་ཚེ་དེ་ལ་ཆོས་ཐམས་ཅད་དེ་བཞིན་ཉིད་དུ་སྣང་བ་ལས་ཐ་དད་པ་དང་། མ་དག་པ་མེད་པས་རང་སྣང་དག་པ་འབའ་ཞིག་གི་ཁྱད་པར་བྱས་ཏེ་སྣང་བ་ཡིན་ནའང་། གནས་མ་གྱུར་པ་རྣམས་ཀྱི་སྣང་ངོ་ལ་དེ་ཉིད་སྟོན་པ་དང་བསྟན་པ་ལ་སོགས་པ་ཐ་དད་པའི་ཚུལ་དུ་འཆར་བ་ཡིན་ནོ། །

Since no phenomenon of any sort whatsoever exists that is not included within the dharmadhatu,[30] the transformed qualities present within the untainted expanse when transformation has been undergone are inconceivable in number, covering in their extent the entire phenomenal world in all its aspects. Here, however, they are presented in terms of the following three:

- The transformation of the vessel and, by force of that, everything appearing as bodies; this is the attainment of dharmakaya,[31] the omnipresent suchness in which there is neither a center nor outer boundaries.
- The transformation of everything included under the process of speech, as exemplified by the sutras; this is the attainment of sambhogakaya,[32] the mastery of the melodious sound of Dharma in an uninterrupted flow and of qualities knowing no end.
- The transformation of that which comprises mind, namely, the all-inclusive base and the sevenfold collection supported by it; this is the attainment of nirmanakaya,[33] whose field of experience consists of the five forms of wisdom.

Alternatively, the specific features [of these three transformations] should be viewed, in respective order, as consisting of the appearances comprising completely pure domains and bodies; the imparting of genuine Dharma instruction; and the revelation of all aspects of knowledge through the wisdom of simplicity and that of complexity.

Furthermore, in the context where the transformation has not been undergone, anything possessing form and any sound characterized as speech qualify as appearances shared in common, whereas mind is not experienced in common. When the transformation has been undergone, however, all phenomena are nothing other than manifestations of the suchness and there is no impurity involved. For that reason, they are appearances demonstrating the specific feature of being exclusively pure self-manifestation.[34]

Nevertheless, in the eyes of those who have not undergone transformation, the one who has achieved that transformation will be experienced in a fashion involving differentiation, where he is seen as being a teacher distinct from his teaching and so on.

གསུམ་པ།

> གང་ཟག་དག་ལ་འཇུག་པ་ནི།
>
> དང་པོ་གཉིས་ནི་སངས་རྒྱས་དང་།
>
> བྱང་ཆུབ་སེམས་དཔའ་རྣམས་ཀྱི་ནི།
>
> དེ་བཞིན་ཉིད་ཡོངས་གྱུར་པ་སྟེ།
>
> ཕྱི་མ་ཉན་ཐོས་རྣམས་དང་ནི།
>
> རང་སངས་རྒྱས་ཀྱི་ཡང་ཡིན་ནོ།

གང་ཟག་གི་གནས་གྱུར་པ་དག་ལ་འཇུག་པ་ནི། གཞད་མ་ཐག་པའི་གནས་གྱུར་དང་པོ་གཉིས་ནི་སངས་རྒྱས་དང་བྱང་ཆུབ་སེམས་དཔའ་རྣམས་ཀྱི་ནི་ཡུལ་དུ་གྱུར་པའི་དེ་བཞིན་ཉིད་གནས་ཡོངས་སུ་གྱུར་པ་སྟེ། སྐུ་གསུམ་ལྟར་ན་ཆོས་སྐུ་ནི་སངས་རྒྱས་ཉིད་ཀྱི་ཡུལ་དང་། ལོངས་སྐུ་ནི་བྱང་ཆུབ་སེམས་དཔའི་ཡུལ་དུ་གྱུར་པའོ། །

ཞིང་ཁམས་དང་ལུས་ཡོངས་སུ་དག་པ་དང་དམ་པའི་ཆོས་ཚད་མེད་པའི་སྣང་བ་ལ་དབང་འབྱོར་པ་ནི་སངས་རྒྱས་དང་བྱང་ཆུབ་སེམས་དཔའ་རྣམས་ལ་ཡོད་ཀྱི་ཉན་ཐོས་ལ་མེད་པའི་ཕྱིར་རོ། །

3) The individuals

> *The approach as related to individuals:*
> *The first two of these are transformations to suchness*
> *Pertaining to buddhas as well as to bodhisattvas;*
> *The last of these pertains additionally*
> *To Shravakas as well as Pratyekabuddhas.*

The approach as related to the *individuals* who undergo transformation *to suchness,* is as follows: *The first two of these transformations* just explained comprise the sphere of experience *of buddhas as well as bodhisattvas.* This is because, of the three kayas, it is the dharmakaya that serves [fully and perfectly] as the object of experience for buddhas alone, while the sambhogakaya is also the object for bodhisattvas. This, in turn, is because buddhas and bodhisattvas possess mastery over the countless appearances of pure domains, utterly pure bodies and genuine Dharma, but Shravakas do not.

ཕྱི་མ་སེམས་ཀྱི་གནས་གྱུར་འདི་ནི་ཉན་ཐོས་རྣམས་དང་ནི་རང་སངས་རྒྱས་ཀྱི་ཡང་ཡིན་ནོ་ཞེས་ཇི་ལྟར་ཞེ་ན་སྐུ་གསུམ་གྱི་དབང་དུ་བྱས་ན་ཉན་རང་རྣམས་ཀྱིས་ཀྱང་རྣམ་པ་ཐམས་ཅད་པའི་ཡེ་ཤེས་མངའ་བའི་སྤྲུལ་སྐུ་མཐོང་ནུས་པའམ། ཡང་ན་དེ་དག་གི་ཀུན་གཞིའི་སྟེང་གི་ཉོན་མོངས་པའི་ཡིད་གནས་གྱུར་པའི་ཆ་ནས་ཕྱི་མ་དེའི་ཆ་ཙམ་ཡོད་པ་ཡིན་པས། ཕྱི་མ་འདི་འཕགས་པ་བཞི་པོའི་ཡང་ཐུན་མོང་ལྟ་བུར་གསུངས་མོད་ཀྱི་འོན་ཀྱང་ཉན་རང་ལ་སེམས་ཀྱི་གནས་གྱུར་ཡོངས་སུ་རྫོགས་པ་མེད་དོ། །

གཞི་པ།

ཁྱད་པར་ཅན་ལ་འཇུག་པ་ནི།
སངས་རྒྱས་བྱང་ཆུབ་སེམས་དཔའ་རྣམས།
ཞིང་ཡོངས་དག་པའི་ཁྱད་པར་དང་།
ཆོས་སྐུ་ལོངས་སྤྱོད་རྫོགས་པ་དང་།
སྤྲུལ་སྐུ་ཐོབ་པས་གཟིགས་པ་དང་།
འདོམས་པ་དང་ནི་དབང་འབྱོར་ཉིད།
ཐོབ་པའི་ཁྱད་པར་ལས་ཡིན་ནོ།

གནས་ཡོངས་སུ་གྱུར་པ་ཁྱད་པར་ཅན་ལ་འཇུག་པ་ནི། སངས་རྒྱས་དང་བྱང་ཆུབ་སེམས་དཔའ་རྣམས་ཀྱི་གནས་གྱུར་ཏེ། གང་གིས་ན་བདག་མེད་གཉིས་ཡོངས་སུ་རྫོགས་པའི་རྣམ་པར་མི་རྟོག་པའི་ཡེ་ཤེས་ཀྱི་མཐུས་གནས་གྱུར་མཐར་ཐུག་ཐོབ་པའི་ཕྱིར་རོ། །

The last of these, the transformation of mind, *pertains additionally to Shravakas and Pratyekabuddhas.*[35] How is this to be understood?

In terms of the three kayas, it means that also Shravakas and Pratyekabuddhas are able to see a nirmanakaya form embodying the wisdom that embraces all aspects.[36] Nevertheless, this last is, in their case, merely partial in the sense that what they have undergone is a transformation of the afflicted mentality, whose orientation is towards the all-inclusive base. This transformation of mind is, therefore, taught to be common to all four types of noble beings to a certain degree, although it is not fully complete in the case of Shravakas and Pratyekabuddhas.

4) The special traits

The introduction to traits especially advanced
Pertains to buddhas as well as to bodhisattvas:
The distinguishing trait of totally pure domains;
That which is gained through attaining the dharmakaya;
Sambhogakaya; as well as nirmanakaya—
The insight, instruction, and consummate mastery—
Are attainments distinctively greater comparatively.

The introduction to the *traits* of those transformations which can be characterized as *especially advanced, pertains to* those attained by *buddhas as well as bodhisattvas.* And why is that? It is because these are ultimate transformations, which they have attained through the efficacy of nonconceptual wisdom, the full completion of freedom from self-entity in both its forms.

དེ་ཧི་ལྟར་ཞེ་ན་ཆོས་ཐམས་ཅད་ཐམས་ཅད་ནས་ཐམས་ཅད་དུ་གནས་གྱུར་པའམ་མངོན་པར་བྱང་ཆུབ་པའམ། མྱ་ངན་ལས་འདས་པའི་རང་བཞིན་དུ་སྣང་བའི་ཕྱིར། ནམ་མཁའི་མཐས་གཏུག་པར་ཞིང་ཡོངས་སུ་དག་པའི་ཁྱད་པར་དང་ཆོས་ཀྱི་སྐུ་དང་། ལོངས་སྤྱོད་རྫོགས་པ་དང་། སྤྲུལ་སྐུ་གསུམ་པོ་ཐོབ་པས་རིམ་པ་ལྟར། ཤེས་བྱ་ཀུན་ལ་ཡེ་ཤེས་ཀྱི་གཟིགས་པ་རྣམ་པར་དག་པ་དང་། ཟབ་ཅིང་རྒྱ་ཆེ་བའི་ཆོས་རྨད་དུ་བྱུང་བ་ཐེག་པ་ཆེན་པོ་འདོམས་པར་མཛད་པ་དང་ནི། མངོན་ཤེས་སོགས་ཀྱི་མཐུ་ཐོགས་པ་མེད་པ་ཐོབ་པས་གཞན་གྱི་དོན་ལ་ཇི་ལྟར་བཞེད་པ་བཞིན་མངའ་དབང་འབྱོར་བ་ཉིད་ཐོབ་པའི་ཁྱད་པར་ལས་ནི་ཉན་རང་ལས་འཕགས་པ་ཡིན་ནོ། །

ལྔ་པ།

དགོས་པ་རྟོགས་ལ་འཇུག་པ་ནི།
སྔོན་གྱི་སྨོན་ལམ་ཁྱད་པར་དང་།
ཐེག་པ་ཆེན་པོ་སྟོན་པ་ནི།
དམིགས་པའི་ཁྱད་པར་ས་བཅུ་ལ།
རབ་ཏུ་སྦྱོར་བའི་ཁྱད་པར་རོ།

གནས་ཡོངས་སུ་གྱུར་པ་ཁྱད་པར་ཅན་དེ་ལ་དགོས་པའམ་མགོ་བའི་རྒྱུ་ཉིད་དུ་གྱུར་པ་གང་ཡིན་པ་རྟོགས་པའམ་ཤེས་པར་བྱ་བ་ལ་འཇུག་པ་ནི། བླ་ན་མེད་པའི་བྱང་ཆུབ་ཆེན་པོ་ཐོབ་པར་འདོད་པས་དེ་ཡི་དོན་དུ་སྨོན་ལམ་བཏབ་པ་སྟེ། བྱང་ཆུབ་སེམས་དཔའི་སྨོན་

If one asks why they are ultimate, it is because they are manifestations of that nature which is nirvana, the transcendence of suffering; they are direct enlightenment, the transformation of all phenomena for every and all time.

The distinguishing trait of totally pure domains extending throughout the reaches of space; and *that which is gained through attaining the dharmakaya,* namely, original wisdom's pure *insight* into all objects of knowledge; that gained through attaining *sambhogakaya,* namely, the gift of imparting *instruction* in the remarkably profound and vast teachings of the Mahayana; *and* that gained through attaining *nirmanakaya,* namely, *consummate mastery* over benefiting others in accordance with their enlightened intention due to their attainment of unhindered magical powers such as extra-sensory perception and so on, *are attainments distinctively greater comparatively* than those of the Shravakas and Pratyekabuddhas.

5) The requirements

The introduction to realizing what is required:
The distinguishing factor of previous wishing prayers;
The distinguishing factor of Mahayana teaching
As focal point; and the further distinguishing factor
Of effective application to all ten levels.

The fifth point is *the introduction to realizing*—which in this case means understanding—*what is required* for this extraordinary transformation, what are the prerequisites. These include *the distinguishing factor of previous wishing prayers* offered by one wishing to attain unsurpassable great

ལམ་ཆེན་པོ་བཅུ་ལ་སོགས་པ་སྟོན་གྱི་སློན་ལམ་གྱི་ཁྱད་པར་དང་། ཐེག་པ་ཆེན་པོའི་ལམ་དང་འབྲས་བུ་སྟོན་པ་ཡི་ཟབ་ཅིང་རྒྱ་ཆེ་བའི་གསུང་རབ་མཐའ་དག་ལ་དམིགས་པའི་སྒོ་ནས་ཤེས་བྱ་བདེན་པ་གཉིས་ལ་སྒྲོ་འདོགས་ཆོད་པའི་ཁྱད་པར་དང་། སྤང་རྟོགས་མཐར་ཕྱིན་པར་སྒྲུབ་པའི་ཆེད་དུ་ས་བཅུ་ལ་གོང་ནས་གོང་དུ་རབ་ཏུ་སྦྱོར་བའི་ཁྱད་པར་དང་གསུམ་གྱིས་ཉན་རང་གི་ལམ་ལས་འཕགས་པའི་གནས་གྱུར་མཐར་ཐུག་པ་དེའི་རྒྱུ་གཏན་ལ་དབབ་པར་བྱའོ། །དེ་ནི་དགོས་པའི་ཁྱད་པར་རོ། །

དྲུག་པ་རྟེན་ལ་མདོར་བསྟན་རྒྱས་བཤད་གཉིས་ལས། དང་པོ།

གནས་སམ་རྟེན་ལ་འཇུག་པ་ནི།
རྣམ་པར་མི་རྟོག་ཡེ་ཤེས་ལ།
འཇུག་པ་རྣམ་པ་དྲུག་གིས་ཏེ།
དམིགས་དང་མཚན་མ་སྤངས་པ་དང་།
ཡང་དག་པ་ཡི་སྦྱོར་བ་དང་།
མཚན་ཉིད་དང་ནི་ཕན་ཡོན་དང་།
ཡོངས་སུ་ཤེས་ལ་འཇུག་པས་སོ།

གནས་ཡོངས་སུ་གྱུར་པ་མཐར་ཐུག་དེའི་གནས་སམ་གཞིའམ་རྟེན་ཉིད་དུ་གྱུར་པའི་ཚུལ་ལ་འཇུག་པ་ནི། རྣམ་པར་མི་རྟོག་པའི་ཡེ་ཤེས་ལ་འཇུག་པ་ཡིན་ཏེ། གང་གི་ཕྱིར་ཞེ་ན་ཡེ་ནས་རྣམ་པར་དག་པའི་གནས་ལུགས་དེ་བཞིན་ཉིད་ཀྱི་དོན་མངོན་དུ་གྱུར་ཅིང་དེའི་

enlightenment where, in praying to do so, the *Ten Great Prayers of a Bodhisattva* and others are offered; *the distinguishing factor of* eliminating overestimation[37] with respect to any object of knowledge comprising the two truths, which is done by taking *as* the *focal point* all scriptures *teaching the Mahayana* path and fruition, whether composed in the vast or profound mode; *and the further distinguishing factor of effective application to all ten* bodhisattva *levels,* such that these are progressively traversed for the sake of accomplishing ultimate relinquishment and realization. One should clearly understand that these three factors are the causes of the ultimate transformation, which is superior to that attained through the paths of the Shravakas and Pratyekabuddhas. That is why these three are the distinctive factors comprising the requirements.

6) The ground

a) The brief presentation
b) The expansion on these six points

a) The brief presentation

The introduction involving the ground or support
Is into original nonconceptual wisdom
As this is approached in a manner involving six points,
Since the focal requirement, attributes surrendered,
The correct way to apply the mind in practice,
The defining characteristics and benefits,
And full understanding are hereby introduced.

The introduction involving the ground[38] *or support* for this ultimate transformation *is the* introduction *into original nonconceptual wisdom.* If one asks why, it is because the transformation consists in actualization of the suchness itself, the abiding nature completely pure from the outset, as well as

རང་བཞིན་དུ་བྱེད་པ་ལ་དེ་ཉིད་ཇི་བཞིན་པར་རྟོགས་པའི་མི་རྟོག་ཡེ་ཤེས་ཉིད་ཀྱི་སྒོ་ནས་ཐོབ་དགོས་ཀྱི། གཞན་དུ་ནམ་ཡང་མི་ཐོབ་པའི་ཕྱིར། དེ་ནི་དེ་འཐོབ་པའི་རྟེན་ཡིན་པའི་ཕྱིར་རོ། །

མི་རྟོག་ཡེ་ཤེས་དེ་ཅི་ལྟ་བུ་ཞེ་ན་དེའི་ཚུལ་ཕྱིན་ཅི་མ་ལོག་པར་གཏན་ལ་འབེབ་པ་ལ་འཇུག་པ་རྣམ་པ་དྲུག་གིས་ཏེ། གང་ཞེ་ན་གང་ལ་དམིགས་ནས་དེ་སྐྱེད་པའི་དམིགས་པ་ལ་འཇུག་པ་དང་། ཡེ་ཤེས་དེ་ཡི་མི་མཐུན་ཕྱོགས་མཚན་མ་སྤངས་པ་ལ་འཇུག་པ་དང་། ཡེ་ཤེས་དེ་ཉིད་རྒྱུད་ལ་བསྐྱེད་ཚུལ་ཡང་དག་པ་ཡི་སྦྱོར་བ་ལ་འཇུག་པ་དང་། ཡེ་ཤེས་དེ་ཡི་བྱེད་ལས་སམ་སྤྱོད་ཡུལ་གྱི་མཚན་ཉིད་ཅི་ལྟ་བུ་ཡིན་པ་ལ་འཇུག་པ་དང་ནི་ཡེ་ཤེས་དེ་ལ་བརྟེན་པའི་ཕན་ཡོན་ལ་འཇུག་པ་དང་། ཡེ་ཤེས་དེ་ཡི་རང་གི་ངོ་བོ་ཅི་ལྟ་བུ་ཡིན་པ་ཡོངས་སུ་ཤེས་ལ་འཇུག་པས་སོ། །

the ability to remain in this natural state.[39] And these require nonconceptual wisdom, which realizes this nature just as it is; otherwise it would remain inaccessible.

If one asks what *this* nonconceptual original wisdom is, securing firm and unmistaken understanding of its character *is approached in a manner involving six points, since* the factors *hereby introduced are*:

i) *The focal requirement,* meaning that which, when focused on, gives rise to this wisdom
ii) How the *attributes* unfavorable to such wisdom are *surrendered*
iii) *How to apply the mind correctly in practice*, the description of how to actually develop[40] wisdom in the mindstream
iv) The *defining characteristics* of wisdom in terms of its effects, that is to say, the sphere of experience it opens
v) The description of the *benefits* based on such wisdom
vi) The *full understanding* of its very essence.

གཉིས་པ་ལ་མདོར་བསྟན་གྱི་རིམ་པ་དང་མཐུན་པར་དེ་དྲུག་པོ་བཤད་པ་ལས། དང་པོ།

དེ་ལ་དང་པོ་དམིགས་པ་ལ།
འཇུག་པ་རྣམ་པ་བཞིར་ཤེས་བྱ།
ཐེག་པ་ཆེན་པོ་སྟོན་པ་དང་།
དེ་ལ་མོས་དང་ངེས་པ་དང་།
ཚོགས་ནི་ཡོངས་སུ་རྫོགས་པས་སོ།

དེ་ལ་དང་པོ་དམིགས་པ་ལ་འཇུག་པ་ནི་རྣམ་པ་བཞིར་ཤེས་པར་བྱ་སྟེ། ཐེག་པ་ཆེན་པོ་སྟོན་པ་ཡི་གཞུང་ཟབ་ཅིང་རྒྱ་ཆེ་བ་ལ་དམིགས་དགོས་ལ། དེ་ཡང་ཐེག་པ་ཆེན་པོའི་བཤེས་གཉེན་བསྟེན་ནས་གདམས་པ་ཕྱིན་ཅི་མ་ལོག་པ་མཉན་པར་བྱ་བ་དང་། དེ་ལ་མོས་པ་མཆོག་ཏུ་བྱ་བ་དང་། དེའི་དོན་ལ་རིགས་པ་བཞིས་ཐེ་ཚོམ་མེད་པའི་ངེས་པ་སྐྱེད་པ་དང་། ངེས་པའི་དོན་བཞིན་ཡིད་ལ་བྱེད་པའི་སྒོ་ནས་ཚོགས་ནི་ཡོངས་སུ་རྫོགས་པར་བྱས་པ་དང་བཞིས་རྣམ་པར་མི་རྟོག་པའི་ཡེ་ཤེས་སྐྱེད་པར་བྱ་སྟེ། དམིགས་པ་དེ་བཞིའི་གང་རུང་ཞིག་མ་ཚང་ན་ཡང་དེ་ཚུལ་བཞིན་མི་སྐྱེ་བར་ཤེས་པས་དེ་བཞིན་དུ་བྱ་བར་གདམས་སོ། །

b) The expansion on these six points

i) The focal requirement

The first of these, the focal requirement,
Should be known to be introduced in four points,
Since what is required is Mahayana teachings,
Commitment to these, along with certitude
And fully completing the two accumulations.

The first of these, the focal requirement, should be known to be introduced in four points, since what is required for wisdom to develop *is* to focus on the texts containing the vast and profound dimensions of *the Mahayana teachings* in conjunction with following a spiritual friend who is faithful to the Mahayana and, in so doing, to listen to his or her unerring instructions; to develop supreme *commitment to these;* to develop—through the four types of logic[41]—a *certitude* which is free of doubts with respect to their meaning; to be in the process of *fully completing the two accumulations* through cultivating one's mind in accord with the meaning about which certitude has been gained. One is instructed to proceed in this way because it is important to understand that, when all four requirements have been fulfilled, nonconceptual wisdom will develop; if any of these are missing, it will not develop correctly.

གཉིས་པ།

གཉིས་པ་མཚན་མ་སྤངས་པ་ལ།
འཇུག་པ་ཡང་ནི་རྣམ་བཞི་སྟེ།
མི་མཐུན་པ་དང་གཉེན་པོ་དང་།
དེ་བཞིན་ཉིད་དང་རྟོགས་པ་ཡི།
མཚན་མ་དག་ནི་སྤངས་པས་སོ།
འདིས་ནི་རིམ་པ་ཇི་ལྟ་བཞིན།
རགས་དང་འབྲིང་དང་ཕྲ་མོ་དང་།
རིང་དུ་རྗེས་སུ་འབྲེལ་བ་ཡི།
མཚན་མ་ཡོངས་སུ་སྤངས་པ་ཡིན།

གཉིས་པ་རློམ་སེམས་ཀྱི་མཚན་མ་སྤངས་པ་ལ་འཇུག་པ་ཡང་ནི་རྣམ་པ་བཞི་སྟེ། འདོད་ཆགས་སོགས་མི་མཐུན་པ་ཡི་ཕྱོགས་ལ་ཞེན་པའི་མཚན་མ་དང་། སྤྱོང་བྱེད་ཀྱི་གཉེན་པོ་མི་སྡུག་པ་སོགས་ལ་ཞེན་པའི་མཚན་མ་དང་། དམིགས་པ་དེ་བཞིན་ཉིད་ལ་ཞེན་པའི་མཚན་མ་དང་། ཡུལ་ཅན་རྟོགས་པའམ་ལམ་གྱི་འབྲས་བུ་ཡང་དག་པའི་ལྟ་བ་དང་སྟོབས་བཅུ་ལ་སོགས་པའི་རྟོགས་པ་ཡི་ཆོས་ལ་ཞེན་པའི་མཚན་མ་དག་ནི་ཡེ་ཤེས་ཀྱི་མི་མཐུན་ཕྱོགས་སུ་གྱུར་པའི་རྟོག་པ་ཡིན་ལ། དེ་དག་རྣམ་པར་སྤངས་པས་ཡེ་ཤེས་དེ་ཡོངས་སུ་དག་པ་ཐོབ་ཞེས་སོ། །

ii) Surrendering attributes

The second, which treats of surrendering attributes,
Is also introduced by way of four points,
Since what is unfavorable and the remedies,
The suchness as well as the realization of this
Are attributes whose surrender leads the way.
By doing this in respective order as follows—
The coarse and the middling, followed by those which are fine,
And those which persist for a very long time indeed—
These attributes are surrendered entirely.

The second, which treats of surrendering the *attributes* associated with a pretentious attitude, *is also introduced by way of four points, since* there *are* four such *attributes* to be surrendered, namely, the attribute of clinging to *what is unfavorable,* meaning such factors as desirous attachment and so on; the attribute of clinging to *the remedies* through which the former are relinquished, such as the idea of repulsiveness[42] and so on; the attribute of clinging to the focal object, *the suchness; as well as* the attribute of clinging to the ten powers and other factors accompanying *realization,* such as clinging to there being someone realizing, a correct view resulting from the path, and so on.

All of these conceptual patterns are unfavorable to actualizing original wisdom, and that is why it has been taught that *surrendering* them *leads the way* to the attainment of wisdom in its full purity.

མཚན་མ་བཞི་སྤྲངས་པ་འདིས་ནི་གོང་གི་རིམ་པ་ཇི་ལྟ་བ་བཞིན་དུ། རགས་པ་དང་འབྲིང་དང་ཕྲ་མོ་དང་ཡུན་རིང་དུ་བདག་གི་རྒྱུད་ལ་རྗེས་སུ་འབྲེལ་བ་ཡི་མཚན་མ་སྤྲང་དཀའ་བའི་བར་དུ་རིམ་བཞིན་ཡོངས་སུ་སྤྲངས་པའི་ཚུལ་བརྗོད་པ་ཡིན་ཏེ། རྣམ་པར་མི་རྟོག་པའི་གཟུངས་བསྟན་པའི་མདོ་ལས་གསུངས་པ་བཞིན་ནོ། །

དེ་ལ་གནས་ངན་ལེན་པའི་རྒྱུ་ཆགས་སོགས་ཀུན་ནས་ཉོན་མོངས་པའི་ཆོས་སུ་གྱུར་པ་རྣམས་ནི་རྟོགས་སླ་ཞིང་ཡིད་འབྱུང་སླ་བའི་ཕྱིར་མི་མཐུན་ཕྱོགས་ལ་ཞེན་པའི་མཚན་མ་ནི་རགས་པ་སྟེ་དང་པོར་སྤྲོང་ངོ་། །

དེའི་གཉེན་པོ་མི་སྡུག་པ་སོགས་ལ་ཡོན་ཏན་དུ་ལྟ་བས་མཚན་མ་འབྲིང་པོ་སྟེ་སྟ་མའི་རྗེས་སུ་སྤྲོང་ངོ་། །

དེ་བཞིན་ཉིད་ནི་སྤང་བྱ་ཀུན་གྱི་གཉེན་པོ་བླ་ན་མེད་པ་ཡིན་པ་དང་རྟོགས་བྱའི་དམ་པ་ཡིན་པས་དེ་ལ་ཞེན་ཅིང་མཚན་མར་འཛིན་པ་ནི་རྟོག་པ་ཕྲ་མོ་སྤྲང་དཀའ་བ་སྟེ་སྟ་མའི་རྗེས་སུ་སྤྲོང་ངོ་། །

རྟོག་པ་ལ་ཞེན་པའི་མཚན་མ་ནི་ཐམས་ཅད་ཀྱི་རྗེས་སུ་སྤྲོང་སྟེ། དེ་ནི་ས་དང་ལམ་གྱི་སྐབས་ན་གོང་མའི་རྟོག་པ་ལ་ཐོབ་འདོད་ཀྱི་འདུན་པ་ཕྲ་མོ་མི་འདོར་བས་ཡུན་རིང་དུ་རྗེས་སུ་འབྲེལ་བ་སྟེ་རྣམ་པར་མི་རྟོག་པའི་ཡེ་ཤེས་ཡོངས་སུ་སྨིན་པའི་བར་དུ་རྟོག་པ་ཕྲ་མོའི་ཚུལ་དུ་རྒྱུད་ལ་འབྲེལ་བ་ཡིན་ནོ། །

These four attributes are to be surrendered *in respective order,* that is, in their above order of appearance, which is their progressive order of difficulty. First *the coarse* are to be eliminated, then *the middling, followed by those which are fine and those which persist* in one's own mindstream *for a very long time indeed. Doing* it *this* way is how *the attributes are surrendered entirely,* as taught in the *Sutra Presenting Nonconceptual Retention.*

Because all causes of inappropriate grounding, such as attachment and so on—which constitute the factors associated with complete affliction—are easy to understand and easy to renounce, the attribute of clinging to unfavorable factors is coarse and is hence surrendered first.

Because viewing the remedies for these—the idea of repulsiveness and so on—as ends in themselves[43] is a middling degree of attribution, its elimination succeeds that of the former.

Because the suchness is the unsurpassable remedy for all factors to be relinquished and because it is the actual point to be realized, clinging to it and entertaining attributes in its regard is a subtle degree of conceptualization difficult to let go of and hence surrendered at a later stage than the former.

Of all attributes, that of clinging to realization is surrendered last. It consists of the subtle aspiration connected with wishing to attain a higher realization. Since this is not something to be abandoned for as long as one is traversing the paths and levels, this subtle concept is linked to one's mindstream for a very long time—until nonconceptual original wisdom has reached its full maturation.

གསུམ་པ།

ཡང་དག་པ་ཡི་སྦྱོར་བ་ལ།
འཇུག་པ་ཡང་ནི་རྣམ་བཞི་སྟེ།
དམིགས་པ་ཡི་ནི་སྦྱོར་བ་དང་།
མི་དམིགས་པ་ཡི་སྦྱོར་བ་དང་།
དམིགས་པ་མི་དམིགས་སྦྱོར་བ་དང་།
མི་དམིགས་དམིགས་པའི་སྦྱོར་བའོ།

ཡང་དག་པ་ཡི་སྦྱོར་བ་ལ་འཇུག་པ་དེ་ཡང་ནི་རྣམ་པ་བཞི་སྟེ། དང་པོར་ཆོས་ཐམས་ཅད་སེམས་ཙམ་དུ་དམིགས་པ་ཡི་ནི་སྦྱོར་བ་ལ་འཇུག་པ་དང་། དེ་ལ་བརྟེན་ནས་གཟུང་བ་མི་དམིགས་པ་ཡི་སྦྱོར་བ་ལ་འཇུག་པ་དང་། དེ་ལ་བརྟེན་ནས་གཟུང་བ་ལ་དམིགས་པའམ་འཛིན་པ་ཉིད་ཀྱང་མི་དམིགས་པའི་སྦྱོར་བ་ལ་འཇུག་པ་དང་། དེ་ལ་བརྟེན་ནས་གཟུང་འཛིན་གང་དུའང་མི་དམིགས་པ་དེ་བཞིན་ཉིད་ལ་དམིགས་པའི་སྦྱོར་བ་ལ་འཇུག་པའི་ཚུལ་གྱིས་རྣམ་པར་མི་རྟོག་པའི་ཡེ་ཤེས་སྐྱེད་པ་ཡིན་པ་ཤེས་པར་བྱའོ།

དེ་ལ་ཕྱིའི་དོན་རང་བཞིན་མེད་པར་རྟོགས་སླ་ལ། དེ་ལས་འཛིན་པ་མི་དམིགས་པ་རྟོགས་དཀའ་བ་སོགས་ཀྱི་ཕྱིར་གོ་རིམ་བཞིན་དུ་རྒྱུད་ལ་སྐྱེད་ཚུལ་ཏེ། དྲོད་སྣང་བ་ཐོབ་པའི་ཏིང་ངེ་འཛིན་སོགས་སུ་གསུངས་པ་དང་ཚུལ་འདྲའོ། །

iii) How to apply the mind correctly in practice

The introduction to practicing wisdom correctly
Entails the following four specific aspects:
Practice involving something to focus on;
Practice involving nothing to focus on;
Practice involving no subject to focus on;
Practice whose focus is nothing to focus on.

The introduction to practicing wisdom correctly entails the following four specific aspects. The first is to engage in *practice involving something to focus on*, namely, that all phenomena are mind only. With that as the basis, one engages in *practice involving nothing* existing that could constitute a perceived object *on* which *to focus.* With that as the basis, one engages in *practice involving no subject to focus on,* i.e., where there is no perceiver in relation to something perceived at all. With that as the basis, one engages in *practice whose focus is* the suchness, in which there is *nothing* of perceived and perceiver *on* which to *focus* at all. One should know that this is how nonconceptual original wisdom is discovered.

The order of these corresponds to their progressive order of development in the mindstream, since it is easier to understand that outer objects do not have a substantial makeup than to understand the more difficult point of there being no perceiver on which to focus and so on, as has been taught in *The Samadhi Wherein the Appearance of Heat is Attained* and elsewhere.

བཞི་པ།

དེ་ལ་མཚན་ཉིད་འཇུག་པ་ནི།
རྣམ་པ་གསུམ་གྱིས་ཤེས་བྱ་སྟེ།

ཆོས་ཉིད་གནས་པ་ཉིད་ལས་ནི།
གཉིས་སུ་མེད་ཅིང་བརྗོད་མེད་པའི།
ཆོས་ཉིད་རབ་ཏུ་གནས་ཕྱིར་རོ།

སྣང་བ་མེད་ལས་གཉིས་དང་ནི།
ཇི་ལྟར་མངོན་པར་བརྗོད་པ་དང་།
དབང་པོ་ཡུལ་དང་རྣམ་རིག་དང་།
སྣོད་ཀྱི་འཇིག་རྟེན་སྣང་མེད་ཕྱིར།
དེས་ན་འདིས་ནི་བརྟག་མེད་པ།
བསྟན་དུ་མེད་པ་གནས་མེད་པ།
སྣང་བ་མེད་ཅིང་རྣམ་རིག་མེད།
གནས་མེད་པ་ཞེས་བྱ་བ་སྟེ།
རྣམ་པར་མི་རྟོག་ཡེ་ཤེས་ཀྱི།
མཚན་ཉིད་མདོ་བཞིན་བརྗོད་པ་ཡིན།

iv) The defining characteristics of wisdom in terms of its effects—the sphere of experience it opens

The defining characteristics here encountered
Should be known to consist of the following three aspects,

Since one effect is repose in pure being,
Which means that one actually settles in pure being,
The non-dualistic and inexpressible;

And one effect relates to appearances' absence,
Where duality, assumption and formulation,
Faculties, objects, principles of awareness,
And vessel-like worlds' appearances are absent;
So these correspond to there being no observation,
No description, no ground and no appearances,
No principles of awareness, and no place,
Which is how the sutras express the traits
Defining original nonconceptual wisdom;

སྣང་བ་ལས་ནི་ཆོས་ཐམས་ཅད།
ནམ་མཁའི་དཀྱིལ་མཉམ་སྣང་ཕྱིར་རོ།
འདུ་བྱེད་ཐམས་ཅད་སྒྱུ་མ་སོགས།
ལྟ་བུར་སྣང་བ་ཡིན་ཕྱིར་རོ།

དེ་ལ་མཚན་ཉིད་ལ་འཇུག་པ་ནི་རྣམ་པ་གསུམ་གྱིས་ཤེས་པར་བྱ་སྟེ། ཆོས་ཉིད་རང་གི་ངོ་བོ་ལ་གནས་པའི་མཚན་ཉིད་དང་། དེ་ལ་སྣང་མེད་དུ་བཞག་པའི་མཚན་ཉིད་དང་། སྣང་བཅས་སུ་བཞག་པའི་མཚན་ཉིད་དོ། །

དང་པོ་ཆོས་ཐམས་ཅད་ཀྱི་ཆོས་ཉིད་དེ་བཞིན་ཉིད་ལ་གནས་པ་ཉིད་ལས་ནི། གཟུང་འཛིན་གཉིས་སམ་ཡང་ན་བདེན་པ་གཉིས་སུ་བློས་དབྱེར་མེད་ཅིང་ངག་གིས་མཐའ་འམ་རྣམ་པ་གང་དུའང་བརྗོད་དུ་མེད་པའི་ཆོས་ཉིད་ལ་རབ་ཏུ་གནས་པའི་ཕྱིར་རོ།

དེ་ཡང་མཐར་ཐུག་པ་ནི་མདེན་གཉིས་དབྱེར་མེད་རོ་གཅིག་ཏུ་ཐུགས་སུ་ཆུད་པ་སངས་རྒྱས་ཀྱི་ཡེ་ཤེས་ཀྱིས་དེ་ཇི་ལྟ་བ་བཞིན་དུ་གཟིགས་ལ་སློབ་ལམ་ན་དེ་ཡི་རྗེས་སུ་མཐུན་པ་ཡོད་པའོ། །

གཉིས་པ་མི་རྟོག་པའི་ཡེ་ཤེས་སྣང་བ་མེད་པ་ཉིད་ཐོབ་པ་ལས་འདི་ལྟར་རྟོག་མེད་དབང་ཤེས་ལ་གཟུང་འཛིན་གཉིས་སུ་སྣང་བ་དང་ནི་གཉིས་སྣང་དེ་ལ་དེར་ཞེན་ནས་རྟོག་པ་དང་བཅས་པའི་ཡིད་ཀྱིས་ཇི་ལྟར་སྣང་བ་དེ་ལ་དེ་དང་དེར་མངོན་པར་བརྗོད་པ་སྟེ། ནང་གི་བརྗོད་པའམ་ཡིད་ཀྱིས་གཟུང་འཛིན་དུ་རྟོག་པ་དང་། མིག་སོགས་ནང་

And one effect relates to appearances' presence,
Since experience of every phenomenon
Is equivalent to the center of open space,
And formations all are appearances like illusions.

The defining characteristics [of the sphere of experience] *here encountered* [as the effect of actualizing nonconceptual wisdom] *should be known to consist of the following three aspects, since* [there are three cases:] the traits of actually settling in the essence of pure being; the traits of placement within that nature when no appearances are experienced; and the traits of a placement involving appearances.

[To look at each of these cases more closely,] *one effect is repose in pure being,* the suchness of all phenomena. This *means* [that one] *actually settles in pure being,* which is *non-dualistic* in that there is no dichotomy of perceived and perceiver and no differentiation of two truths by a discursive intellect. It is also *inexpressible* through any linguistic device or in terms of any extreme whatsoever.

The ultimate case of this is the wisdom of a buddha, which, in comprehending the two truths to be indivisible, i.e., to be of one taste, beholds pure being simply as it is. There is, however, an approximation of this on the path of learning.

And one effect relates to an attainment of nonconceptual wisdom where *appearances* are completely *absent,* that is to say, where the following have in all aspects and in every way subsided:

- What appears to the nonconceptual sensory faculty as a *duality* of perceived and perceiver
- The process of *formulation* conducted by the rational mind, which is conceptual and first makes the *assumption* that whatever appears to be a duality actually exists that way and then formulates it by assigning a specific term; this is a process which is internal and equivalent to the rational mind's conceptualization of percept and perceiver

གི་དབང་པོ་དང་། གཟུགས་སོགས་ཕྱིའི་ཡུལ་དང་། མིག་གི་རྣམ་ཤེས་སོགས་རྣམ་པར་རིག་པ་དང་། ཐུན་མོང་སྣོད་ཀྱི་འཇིག་རྟེན་དུ་སྣང་བ་འདི་དག་ཐམས་ཅད་ནས་ཐམས་ཅད་དུ་ནུབ་སྟེ་མེད་པའི་ཕྱིར་དེ་གང་གིས་ཀྱང་ཁྱད་པར་བྱར་མེད་པའི་དེ་བཞིན་ཉིད་རོ་གཅིག་ཏུ་སྣང་བ་ནི་སྟོང་པ་ཉིད་ལ་གཉིས་སྣང་ནུབ་པ་ཞེས་བྱའོ། །

དེས་ན་བཤད་མ་ཐག་པའི་དོན་དྲུག་བསྟན་པ་འདིས་ནི་རིམ་པ་ལྟར། དབང་པོ་སོགས་ཀྱི་ཤེས་པ་བརྟག་ཏུ་མེད་པ། ངག་གིས་བསྟན་དུ་མེད་པ། ཤེས་པ་སྐྱེ་བའི་གནས་སམ་རྟེན་མེད་པ། ཡུལ་དུ་སྣང་བ་མེད་ཅིང་ཡུལ་ཅན་རྣམ་པར་རིག་པ་མེད་པ། ཐུན་མོང་གི་རྟེན་སྣོད་ཀྱི་གནས་མེད་པ་ཞེས་བྱ་བ་སྟེ། ཚུལ་འདིས་རྣམ་པར་མི་རྟོག་པའི་ཡེ་ཤེས་ཀྱི་མཚན་ཉིད་བསྟན་པ་ཡིན་ལ། དེ་ནི་དེ་བཞིན་གཤེགས་པས་མདོ་ལས་གསུངས་པ་བཞིན་དུ་འདིར་བརྗོད་པ་ཡིན་ནོ། །ཇི་ལྟར་ན་དཀོན་བཚོག་བརྩེགས་པའི་འོད་སྲུང་གིས་ཞུས་པ་ལུང་བསྟན་པ་ལས།

འོད་སྲུང་རྟག་ཅེས་བྱ་བ་འདི་ནི་མཐའ་གཅིག་གོ། །མི་རྟག་ཅེས་བྱ་བ་འདི་ནི་མཐའ་གཉིས་སོ། །མཐའ་དེ་གཉིས་ཀྱི་དབུས་གང་ཡིན་པ་དེ་ནི་དཔྱད་དུ་མེད་པ། བསྟན་དུ་མེད་པ། རྟེན་མ་ཡིན་པ། སྣང་བ་མེད་པ། རྣམ་པར་རིག་པ་མེད་པ། གནས་པ་མེད་པ་སྟེ། འོད་སྲུང་འདི་ནི་དབུ་མའི་ལམ་ཆོས་རྣམས་ལ་ཡང་དག་པར་སོ་སོར་རྟོག་པ་ཞེས་བྱའོ། །

- The inner *faculties*, that of the eye and so on
- Outer *objects*, form and so on
- The *principles of awareness*, the eye consciousness, and so on
- *Vessel-like worlds' appearances* experienced in common.

Since these *are* all *absent*, suchness free of all these types of differentiation appears in its one taste. This is what is referred to as "the subsiding of dualistic appearance into emptiness."

So these six just listed and in the same order *correspond to there being*

- *no* act of *observation*[44] on the part of any consciousness, sensory or otherwise
- *no* linguistic *description*
- no support or *ground* for the incidence of consciousness
- *no appearance* of objects to be observed
- *no principles of awareness* as observer
- as well as *no place* in the form of a vessel as the support for common experience,

which is how the traits defining nonconceptual original wisdom are taught here. This corresponds to the way they are *express*ed in *the sutras* spoken by the Tathagata. For example, in *The Mosaic of the Rare and Supreme Ones, Requested by Kashyapa*, the Buddha taught,

> Kashyapa, "permanence" is one extreme;[45] "impermanence," another. The middle between these two extremes is where there is no analysis,[46] no description, no support, no appearance, no principles of awareness, and no place. Kashyapa, this is the middle path and is called "intimate and detailed discernment of phenomena correctly applied."

ཞེས་དང་དེ་བཞིན་དུ་བདག་བདག་མེད་འཁོར་བ་མྱང་འདས་ཡོད་པ་དང་མེད་པ་སོགས་ལ་སྦྱར་ཏེ་དེ་གཉིས་ཀྱི་དབུས་གང་ཡིན་པ་དེ་ནི་དབྱེར་དུ་མེད་པ་སོགས་གོང་ལྟར་གསུངས་སོ། །

དེའི་ཕྱིར་སྣང་བ་དེ་དག་གི་རང་བཞིན་ལས་འདས་པའི་སྣང་བ་མེད་པའི་ཡེ་ཤེས་རང་འོད་གསལ་བ་ནམ་མཁའ་དང་མཉམ་པ་དེ་ལ་རྣམ་པར་མི་རྟོག་པའི་ཡེ་ཤེས་སྣང་བ་མེད་པ་ཞེས་བྱ་ལ། དེ་རང་གི་ངོ་བོ་ནི་རྣམ་པར་ཤེས་པ་ལས་འདས་པའི་ཡེ་ཤེས་ཡིན་ཏེ་འདུས་བྱས་འདུས་མ་བྱས་སོགས་ཀྱི་ཁམས་གང་དུའང་མ་གཏོགས་པའོ། །

དེའི་ཕྱིར་དེའི་ངོ་བོ་ལ་སྣང་བ་དེ་དག་གིས་རེས་སུ་བཅད་པ་མེད་དེ་ཆོས་ཉིད་དང་གཉིས་སུ་མེད་པར་རང་གསལ་བའོ། །

ཇི་ལྟ་བ་རྟོགས་པའི་ཡེ་ཤེས་ཀྱི་ལྡོག་ཆ་ནས་བསྟན་ན། རྟག་ཏུ་འདིའི་ངང་ཚུལ་ལས་མ་གཡོས་བཞིན་དུ་ཇི་སྙེད་པའི་ཡེ་ཤེས་ཀྱིས་སྣང་བ་ཐམས་ཅད་མཉམ་ལ་མ་འདྲེས་པར་གཟིགས་པ་འབྱུང་སྟེ་འགལ་མེད་ཟུང་གཅིག་ཏུ་རུང་ངོ་། །

དེ་ཅིའི་ཕྱིར་ཞེ་ན། ཆོས་ཉིད་དེ་བཞིན་ཉིད་ཀྱི་ངང་དུ་ཆོས་ཐམས་ཅད་རོ་མཉམ་པ་ལས་མ་གཡོས་བཞིན་དུ་ཆོས་ཅན་ཐམས་ཅད་སྣང་བར་ཟད་ཀྱི་དེ་གཉིས་མི་འགལ་བ་བཞིན་དུ། ཆོས་ཉིད་གཟིགས་པའི་ཡེ་ཤེས་ཀྱི་རང་སྣང་ལ་སྣང་བ་མི་འགག་པར་ཤར་ཡང་དེ་དང་དེར་དམིགས་པ་མེད་པའི་ཆ་ནས་གོང་གི་སྣང་མེད་དུ་བསྟན་པའི་དོན་ཡོངས་སུ་རྫོགས་པ་ཡིན་ཏེ་ཐ་མལ་པའི་གཉིས་སྣང་ལ་སོགས་པའི་རང་བཞིན་ལས་འདས་པའི་ཕྱིར་རོ། །

འདི་ཤིན་ཏུ་གལ་ཆེ་བའི་ཟབ་དོན་དེ་འཕྲོས་སུ་བཤད་པའོ། །

What is taught in the preceding quotation is then related in a similar fashion to self and no self, samsara and nirvana, existence and non-existence, and so on, where the middle between the two in each case is taught as being free of analysis and so forth, as above.

Hence, wisdom devoid of appearances is one which transcends the parameters defining appearance as described above and is itself the clear light, all-pervasive as space. This is called "nonconceptual original wisdom free of appearance." It is essentially beyond consciousness and is thus not restricted to any domain whatsoever, whether that of the composite, the non-composite or any other. Since this means original wisdom itself does not fall into the category of appearances, it is not something distinct from pure being but is its intrinsic luminous clarity.

This wisdom could be explained in terms of its facets. Without ever stirring from the inherent state, which is the wisdom realizing simplicity, the wisdom associated with complexity sees all appearances as equal without mixing them. These two facets of wisdom cooperate in unison without any contradiction.

If one asks how this could be so, while no phenomenon ever wavers from "equal taste" in the depths of suchness, which is pure being, the entire world of phenomena is nothing but appearance. And just as these two [phenomena and suchness] are not in contradiction, appearances—which are the self-manifestation of original wisdom contemplating pure being—manifest without hindrance, even though these do not exist as this and that objective focal referent. From this perspective, the picture of "absence of appearance" presented above is complete, since the dualistic makeup of appearances with everything that ordinarily goes with it[47] is hereby transcended. This profound point has been given the very thorough consideration it deserves because of its immense importance.

གསུམ་པ་སྣང་བ་ལས་ནི་ཇི་ལྟར་ན་མཉམ་བཞག་ཏུ་ནི་ཆོས་ཐམས་ཅད་རོ་མཉམ་པར་དེ་བཞིན་ཉིད་ཀྱི་ངོ་བོས་དམིགས་པར་བྱར་མེད་པ། དཔེར་ན་ནམ་མཁའི་དཀྱིལ་ལྟར་མཉམ་པ་ཉིད་དུ་སྣང་བའི་ཕྱིར་རོ། །

མཉམ་བཞག་དེ་ལྟ་བུའི་རྗེས་ལས་ཐོབ་པའི་ཡེ་ཤེས་ཀྱིས་ནི་འདུ་བྱེད་པའི་ཆོས་ཐམས་ཅད་ཅི་དང་གང་སྣང་བ་མ་ལུས་པ་སྣང་ཡང་རང་བཞིན་མ་གྲུབ་པའི་སྒྱུ་མ་དང་སྨིག་རྒྱུ་དང་རྨི་ལམ་ལ་སོགས་པ་ལྟ་བུར་སྣང་བ་ཡིན་པའི་ཕྱིར་རོ། །

མཉམ་རྗེས་མེད་པར་ཟུང་གཅིག་ཏུ་རྒྱུད་པ་མཐར་ཕྱུག་པ་ནི་སངས་རྒྱས་ཀྱི་སར་འབྱུང་ཞིང་། རྗེས་མཐུན་པ་འཕགས་པའི་ས་དང་ཆ་འདྲ་བ་སློབ་ལམ་གྱི་དཔེ་ཡི་ཡེ་ཤེས་རྒྱུད་ལ་སྐྱེས་པ་ན་ཡང་འབྱུང་སྟེ་ཐབས་ཟབ་པའི་ཕྱིར་རོ། །

ཚུལ་འདིས་མཐར་ཕྱུག་སངས་རྒྱས་ཀྱིས་ཇི་ལྟ་ཇི་སྙེད་ཀྱི་ཡེ་ཤེས་རྣམ་པ་གཉིས་པོས་གཟིགས་ཚུལ་དང་སློབ་ལམ་དུ་མཉམ་བཞག་སྣང་བཅས་སྣང་མེད་མི་འགལ་བའི་གནད་ཤེས་དགོས་པས་ཤིན་ཏུ་གལ་ཆེ་བའི་ཕྱིར་འཕྲོས་དོན་ཙུང་ཟད་དང་བཅས་ཏེ་བཤད་པ་ཡིན་ནོ། །

There is also *one effect* which *relates to appearances' presence.* And how so?

During meditative equipoise, *every phenomenon* is of equal taste in having the essential non-referentiality of the suchness, *since,* to illustrate this with an example, the *experience* of these *is* completely *equivalent to* the experience of *the center of open space.*[48]

And, from the point of view of the wisdom attained in the wake of such an equipoise, i.e., during post-meditation, whatever phenomena consisting of *formations* might appear and however they might do so, none of them verifiably exists with a substantial makeup, even though they appear, *since all* of them *are appearances* that are *like illusions,* mirages, dreams, and so on.

The ultimate achievement of union, in which there is no differentiation between a meditative and post meditative state, occurs at the level of buddhahood. An approximation of this occurs on the levels achieved by noble beings, and there is a partial resemblance to it in a mindstream where the symbolic wisdom of the mantric path has manifested due to profound skillful means.

This is another important point and has therefore required a somewhat detailed explanation, since one needs to understand that there is no contradiction between the ultimate way in which a buddha sees—via the two aspects of original wisdom as associated with simplicity and complexity—and the meditative equipoise of the path of learning, whether this is accompanied by the process of appearance or not.

ལྔ་པ།

ཕན་ཡོན་འཇུག་པ་རྣམ་བཞི་སྟེ།
ཆོས་སྐུ་རྫོགས་པར་ཐོབ་པ་དང་།
གོང་ན་མེད་པའི་བདེ་ཐོབ་དང་།
གཟིགས་པ་དབང་འབྱོར་ཐོབ་པ་དང་།
སྟོན་ལ་དབང་འབྱོར་ཐོབ་པའོ།

མི་རྟོག་པའི་ཡེ་ཤེས་དེ་ཡི་ཕན་ཡོན་ལ་འཇུག་པ་ནི་རྣམ་བཞི་སྟེ། རྣམ་པར་མི་རྟོག་པའི་ཡེ་ཤེས་དེ་ཉིད་ཀྱིས། སྒྲིབ་པ་གཉིས་དང་བྲལ་བའི་གནས་ཡོངས་སུ་གྱུར་པ་མཐར་ཐུག་པ་ཆོས་ཀྱི་སྐུ་རྫོགས་པར་ཐོབ་པ་དང་། འགྱུར་ཞིང་མི་བརྟན་པ་ཟག་བཅས་ཀྱི་བདེ་བ་བག་ཆགས་དང་བཅས་པ་ལས་འདས་ནས་གོང་ན་མེད་པའི་བདེ་བ་ཆེན་པོ་ཟག་པ་མེད་ཅིང་གཏན་དུ་འཕོ་འགྱུར་མེད་པ་ཐོབ་པ་དང་། ཇི་ལྟ་བ་དང་ཇི་སྙེད་པས་བསྡུས་པའི་ཤེས་བྱ་ཐམས་ཅད་ལ་ཕྱིན་ཅི་མ་ལོག་པའི་གཟིགས་པ་རྣམ་པར་དག་པ་ལྷུན་གྱིས་གྲུབ་པ་ལ་དབང་འབྱོར་བ་ཐོབ་པ་དང་། མཐའ་ཡས་པའི་གདུལ་བྱ་ལ་རང་རང་གི་མོས་པ་དང་འཚམས་པའི་ཆོས་ཀྱི་སྒོ་སྣ་ཚོགས་པ་ཟབ་པ་དང་རྒྱ་ཆེ་བའི་ཚུལ་འབད་མེད་དུ་སྟོན་པ་ལ་དབང་འབྱོར་བ་བཞི་ཐོབ་པའོ། །

དེ་ལྟར་ན་སྤང་རྟོགས་མཐར་ཐུག་པ་བསྐྱེད་པའི་རྒྱུ་ནི་རྣམ་པར་མི་རྟོག་པའི་ཡེ་ཤེས་ཉིད་ཡིན་པའི་ཕྱིར་ཡེ་ཤེས་དེའི་ཕན་ཡོན་རྣམ་པ་བཞི་བསྟན་པའོ། །

v) The benefits

The four points introducing the benefits
Include the complete attainment of dharmakaya,
Attainment of bliss which nothing can exceed,
Attainment of mastery over the power of insight,
And attainment of mastery over the power to teach.

There are *four points introducing the benefits* of nonconceptual original wisdom. By virtue of realizing this wisdom, one gains

- *the complete attainment of dharmakaya,* the ultimate transformation, which is free of the two obscurations
- the *attainment*—due to the transcendence of changeable and unstable tainted happiness along with the ingrown habits related to these—*of* an untainted and fundamentally unchanging and unwavering great *bliss which nothing can exceed*
- the *attainment of mastery over the power of* completely pure *insight,* which is spontaneously present and unerring with respect to objects of knowledge, all of which are included under simplicity and complexity
- the *attainment of mastery over the power to* effortlessly *teach,* in the profound as well as the vast mode, the variety of avenues of approach to the Dharma and to do so in a manner that corresponds to the specific inclinations of the individual beings to be tamed, who are infinite in number.

Since the cause for the development of ultimate relinquishment and realization is nonconceptual wisdom, the four points depicting the benefits of this wisdom have been included here.

དྲུག་པ་ཡེ་ཤེས་དེའི་ཚུལ་ཡོངས་སུ་ཤེས་པ་ལ་འཇུག་པ་ལ། མདོར་བསྟན་དང་། རྒྱས་བཤད་གཉིས། དང་པོ།

ཡོངས་སུ་ཤེས་ལ་འཇུག་པ་ནི།
རྣམ་པ་བཞི་རུ་ཤེས་བྱ་སྟེ།
གཉེན་པོ་ཡོངས་སུ་ཤེས་པ་དང་།
མཚན་ཉིད་ཡོངས་སུ་ཤེས་པ་དང་།
ཁྱད་པར་ཡོངས་སུ་ཤེས་པ་དང་།
ལས་ལྔ་ཡོངས་སུ་ཤེས་པའོ།

ཡོངས་སུ་ཤེས་པ་ལ་འཇུག་པ་དེ་ནི་རྣམ་པ་བཞི་རུ་ཤེས་པར་བྱ་སྟེ། མི་མཐུན་ཕྱོགས་ཀྱི་གཉེན་པོ་བྱེད་ཚུལ་ཡོངས་སུ་ཤེས་པ་དང་། གོལ་ས་མི་རྟོག་པ་ལྔ་དང་བྲལ་བའི་ཚུལ་གྱིས་རང་གི་མཚན་ཉིད་ཡོངས་སུ་ཤེས་པ་དང་། དམན་ལམ་ལས་ཁྱད་པར་འཕགས་པའི་ཆོས་ལྔ་ཡོངས་སུ་ཤེས་པ་དང་། ཡེ་ཤེས་དེའི་བྱེད་ལས་ལྔ་ཡོངས་སུ་ཤེས་པ་དང་བཞིའོ། །

vi) The introduction to full understanding

The introduction to a full understanding of the character of this wisdom includes:

(a) The brief presentation
(b) The expansion on that

(a) The brief presentation

The introduction to thorough understanding
Should be known to include the following four points:
A full understanding regarding the remedy;
A full understanding regarding the characteristic;
A full understanding regarding distinctive marks;
And a full understanding regarding the five effects.

The introduction to thorough understanding should be known to include the following four points:

(i) *A full understanding regarding the* way wisdom functions as a *remedy* for unfavorable factors
(ii) *A full understanding* of the concrete *characteristic* of nonconceptual wisdom, gained by eliminating the five instances of pseudo nonconceptuality
(iii) *A full understanding* of the five *distinctive marks* that elevate it above the minor paths
(iv) *And a full understanding* of *the five effects* produced through this wisdom.

གཉིས་པ་རྒྱས་བཤད་ལ་གོང་གི་རིམ་པ་དང་མཚུངས་པར་བཞི་ལས། དང་པོ།

དེ་ལ་གཉེན་པོ་ཤེས་པ་ནི།
རྣམ་པར་མི་རྟོག་ཡེ་ཤེས་ཏེ།
ཆོས་དང་གང་ཟག་འཛིན་པ་དང་།
ཡོངས་གྲུར་པ་དང་ཐ་དད་དང་།
སྐུར་བ་འདེབས་པ་ཉིད་ཡིན་ཏེ།
མེད་པ་འཛིན་པ་རྣམ་པ་ལྔའི།
གཉེན་པོ་བསྟན་པ་ཡིན་ཕྱིར་རོ།

དེ་ལ་གཉེན་པོ་ཤེས་པ་ནི་གང་ཞེ་ན་རྣམ་པར་མི་རྟོག་པའི་ཡེ་ཤེས་དེ་ནི་བདེན་གཉིས་དབྱེར་མེད་ཀྱི་གནས་ལུགས་སྒྲོ་སྐུར་དང་བྲལ་བའི་དེ་བཞིན་ཉིད་ལ་ཞུགས་པའི་ཕྱིར་ན་མཐར་འཛིན་པའི་ལྟ་བ་ངན་པ་ཐམས་ཅད་སེལ་བར་བྱེད་པ་ཡིན་ཏེ། གཟུགས་སོགས་ཀྱི་ཆོས་སུ་འཛིན་པ་དང་། གང་ཟག་གི་བདག་ཏུ་འཛིན་པ་དང་། དངོས་པོ་རྣམས་སྔ་མའི་གནས་སྐབས་ལས་ཡོངས་སུ་གྱུར་པ་སྐྱེ་བ་དང་འགག་པར་འཛིན་པ་དང་། ཆོས་ཅན་དང་ཆོས་ཉིད་ཐ་དད་པར་འཛིན་པ་དང་། སྣང་ཙམ་གྱི་ཆོས་རྣམས་ཐ་སྙད་དུ་མེད་ཅེས་སྐུར་བ་འདེབས་པ་ཉིད་དང་ལྔ་ཡིན་ཏེ། དེ་ལྔ་པོ་ནི་དོན་ལ་དེ་ལྟར་མེད་པའམ་མ་གྲུབ་པ་ཡིན་པ་ལ་རྨོངས་པའི་བློས་བདག་གཉིས་དང་སྐྱེ་འགག་དང་ཐ་དད་དང་སྐུར་འདེབས་ཀྱི་རྣམ་པར་འཛིན་པས་ན་དེ་ཐམས་ཅད་མི་བདེན་པ་ལ་ཞུགས་པས་ན་མེད་པ་འཛིན་པ་ཞེས་བྱ་སྟེ།

(b) The expansion on that

(i) Fully understanding the remedy

What is to be understood as the remedy here
Is nonconceptualizing original wisdom,
Since perceiving phenomena, individuals,
An alteration as well as dichotomy,
Denial as well, when this is entertained,
Are five distinct forms of perception of non-existents
For which it is taught to comprise the remedy.

One might well ask, "*What is to be understood* to play the role of *remedy here*?"

The reply would be, "*Nonconceptual original wisdom.*" Because it rests in suchness, the abiding nature free of overestimation and denial[49] wherein the two truths are inseparable, it eliminates all wrong views, which fixate on theoretical conclusions.[50]

There are five cases to be remedied, *since perceiving phenomena*, such as forms and so on; perceiving a self in connection with *individuals*; perceiving *an* arising and cessation, that is, a complete *alteration* of things in comparison to an earlier stage; perceiving a *dichotomy* between the phenomenal world and pure being; *as well as denial, when this is entertained* through claiming that even the mere appearance of a phenomenon does not exist conventionally, are five cases of something not present and in reality not existing as it seems being perceived by an unclear intellect to take the form of the two types of self-entity, arising and cessation, dichotomy, and denial.

དེ་ལྟར་མེད་པ་འཛིན་པའམ་ཕྱིན་ཅི་ལོག་ཏུ་འཛིན་པ་རྣམ་པ་ལྔའི་གཉེན་པོ་ཉིད་དུ་བསྟན་པ་ནི་རྣམ་པར་མི་རྟོག་པའི་ཡེ་ཤེས་དེ་ཉིད་ཡིན་པའི་ཕྱིར་རོ། རྣམ་པར་མི་རྟོག་པའི་ཡེ་ཤེས་དང་ལྡན་པ་ལ་ཕྱིན་ཅི་ལོག་གི་ལྟ་བ་སྒྲོ་འདོགས་པའི་དང་སྐུར་འདེབས་གཅིག་པོ་དེས་མཚོན་པའི་ལྟ་བ་ངན་པ་མཐའ་དག་འབྱུང་བར་མི་འགྱུར་རོ། །

གཉིས་པ།

མཚན་ཉིད་ཡོངས་སུ་ཤེས་པ་ནི།

ཡིད་ལ་མི་བྱེད་ཡང་དག་འདས།

ཉེ་བར་ཞི་དང་ངོ་བོའི་དོན།

མངོན་རྟགས་འཛིན་པ་རྣམ་པ་ལྔ།

སྤངས་པའི་རང་གི་མཚན་ཉིད་དོ།

མི་རྟོག་ཡེ་ཤེས་ཀྱི་མཚན་ཉིད་ཡོངས་སུ་ཤེས་པ་ནི། མི་མཐུན་ཕྱོགས་གོལ་ས་རྣམ་ལྔ་སྤང་པའི་སྒོ་ནས་བསྟན་ཏེ། དེ་ཅིའི་ཕྱིར་ན་རྣམ་པར་མི་རྟོག་པའི་ཡེ་ཤེས་ནི་དམིགས་པར་བྱ་བའི་རྣམ་པ་ཅི་ཡང་མ་མཐོང་ལ་ཅིར་ཡང་མི་འཛིན་པ་ཡིན་མོད་ཀྱི་དེས་ཆོས་ཐམས་ཅད་ཀྱི་དེ་བཞིན་ཉིད་མཐོང་བ་ཡིན་པའི་ཚུལ་འདི་དཔུས་ལོང་ལ་གཟུགས་ལྟར་རོ། །

Since all of these are cases of involvement in a fiction, they *are* referred to as "*perception of non-existents.*" They are *five distinct forms of* a distorted mode of perception, where the perceiver applies itself to something which does not exist as it seems, *for which it is* precisely nonconceptual wisdom that is *taught to comprise the* sole *remedy.*

Anyone equipped with realization of nonconceptual wisdom will avoid all misguided views, as exemplified by these five mistaken forms of perception—four of which are cases of overestimation, one of denial.

(ii) Fully understanding the concrete characteristic

Full understanding regarding the characteristic:
A lack of the process of thought and correct transcendence,
Tranquilization, things in their composition,
And predetermination are the five
The exclusion of which is the concrete characteristic.

Full understanding regarding *the* concrete *characteristic* of nonconceptual original wisdom is rendered accessible through a process of elimination applied to the five instances of pseudo nonconceptuality, which are not conducive to such wisdom.

The reason for proceeding in this way is that nonconceptual wisdom does not see any image at all that could function as a focal object, nor does it involve any fixation at all. Even though this is indeed the case, it nevertheless "sees" the suchness of all phenomena in a manner which could be likened to the way forms are "seen" by a person blind from birth.

ཆུ་རོལ་མཐོང་བའི་ངོར་སྒྲུབ་པའི་ཚུལ་གྱིས་ཅིག་ཆར་བསྟན་དུ་མེད་པས་དེའི་ངོ་བོ་ཅིར་ཡང་མི་རྟོག་པ་ཡིན་ཀྱང་ཆོས་ཉིད་མཐའ་གང་དུའང་དམིགས་སུ་མེད་པའི་དོན་མ་ནོར་བར་རྟོགས་ནས་ཆོས་ཉིད་དང་མཐུན་པར་ཅིར་ཡང་མི་འཛིན་པ་ཡིན་གྱི། ཅིའང་མ་ཤེས་པའམ་ཤེས་པ་བཀག་པ་སོགས་ཀྱི་སྒོ་ནས་མི་རྟོག་པ་མིན་ནོ་ཞེས་བསྟན་པ་སྟེ། དེ་གང་ཞེ་ན། འཇིག་རྟེན་ཕ་སྐད་ཀྱི་སྦྱོར་བ་རྣམས་མིང་དོན་བསྲེས་ཏེ་རྟོག་པས་ཡིད་ལ་མི་བྱེད་པ་ཙམ་གྱིས་རྣམ་པར་མི་རྟོག་པ་ཞེས་མི་བྱ་སྟེ། བུ་ཆུང་སྐྱེས་མ་ཐག་པ་དང་བེའུ་སོགས་ཀྱི་རྒྱུད་ན་དེ་འདྲའི་རྟོག་པ་མེད་ཀྱང་དེ་ལ་རྣམ་པར་མི་རྟོག་པ་ཞེས་མི་བྱ་བ་བཞིན་ནོ། །

བུ་ཆུང་གི་རྒྱུད་ལ་སྒྲ་དོན་འདྲེས་རུང་ཡོད་དུ་ཆུག་ཀྱང་འདྲེས་འཛིན་མེད་ལ་སྐྱེས་མ་ཐག་པ་རྟོག་དཔྱོད་གཞུག་མི་ཤེས་པ་ལ་དཔེར་བྱས་པས་སྐབས་ཀྱི་དོན་འགྲུབ་བོ། །

རྩིང་ཞིབ་ཀྱི་རྣམ་པ་ཅན་གྱི་རྟོག་དཔྱོད་ལས་ཡང་དག་པར་འདས་པ་ཙམ་གྱིས་ཀྱང་རྣམ་པར་མི་རྟོག་པའི་ཡེ་ཤེས་སུ་མི་འགྱུར་ཏེ་བསམ་གཏན་གཉིས་པ་ཡན་ཆད་ཀྱི་ཤེས་པ་བཞིན་ནོ། །

རྟོག་པ་ཉེ་བར་ཞི་བ་ཙམ་ཞིག་གིས་ཀྱང་དེ་མ་ཡིན་ཏེ་གཉིད་ལོག་པ་དང་བརྒྱལ་བ་དང་མྱོས་པ་དང་འགོག་སྙོམས་ལ་གནས་པའི་གནས་སྐབས་བཞིན་ནོ། །

Because such wisdom cannot be described in an obvious and affirmative fashion for those whose vision is limited to "this shore," its essence [is defined in terms of what it is *not*, namely, it] is not at all conceptual; nevertheless, it unerringly realizes pure being—that reality which does not function as a focal referent and in relation to which no theoretical conclusions are applicable—and does so in a manner not involving fixation at all, as is consistent with pure being.

The cases not conveying what is intended in this context by the term "nonconceptual" include a total absence of consciousness, blocked states of consciousness, and so on, as further elaborated below.

A mere *lack of the process of thought* whereby the elaborations associated with worldly conventions are conceptualized by mixing names with their referents is not what is meant by "nonconceptual," just as there is no such conceptuality in the mindstream of a newly born child or in that of a calf, and so on, without this being what is implied by "nonconceptual" here.

Even though the potential for blending term and referent is present in the mindstream of a child, a newly born is not involved in such a process of associative perception and does not know how to engage in examination and analysis; hence, the example is valid for the case in point.

Mere *correct transcendence* of examination and analysis, characterized respectively as rough and fine, such as the state of consciousness associated with the second level of meditative concentration and upwards,[51] would not be nonconceptual original wisdom either, nor would a mere *tranquilization* of concepts, as in the case of deep sleep, loss of consciousness, inebriation, and the state of repose in the Equilibrium of Cessation.[52]

མི་རྟོག་པའི་ངོ་བོའི་དོན་ཅན་དུ་སྒྱུར་བས་ཀྱང་དེ་མ་ཡིན་དེ་གཟུགས་སོགས་ཡུལ་དང་མིག་སོགས་ཀྱི་དབང་པོ་རྣམས་རྟོག་པ་མེད་པའི་བེམ་པོའི་ངོ་བོར་གྱུར་ཀྱང་དེ་དག་མི་རྟོག་པའི་ཡེ་ཤེས་མ་ཡིན་པའི་ཕྱིར་རོ། །

ཅི་ཡང་རྣམ་པར་རྟོག་པར་མི་བྱའོ་སྙམ་དུ་མངོན་རྟགས་སུ་འཛིན་པ་ཡང་རྣམ་པར་མི་རྟོག་པ་མ་ཡིན་ཏེ་རྟོག་པར་མི་བྱ་སྙམ་དུ་ངེས་ངེས་གསལ་གསལ་གྱི་ཚུལ་དུ་དེ་དང་དེར་མངོན་རྟགས་སུ་འཛིན་པའམ། བཀྲ་བར་འཛིན་པ་དེ་ག་ཁོ་རང་མཚན་མར་འཛིན་པ་ཡིན་པའི་ཕྱིར་རྣམ་པར་མི་རྟོག་པ་མ་ཡིན་པར་འགྱུར་རོ། །

དེ་ལྟ་ན་མི་རྟོག་ཞེས་པའི་སྒྲ་འཇུག་པའི་ཡུལ་རྣམ་པ་ལྔ་ཡི་དང་ཚུལ་དེ་དང་མ་འདྲེས་པར་སྤྱང་པའི་ཚུལ་གྱིས་རྣམ་པར་མི་རྟོག་པའི་ཡེ་ཤེས་རང་གི་མཚན་ཉིད་དེ་ལྟར་བཤད་དོ། །

དེས་ན་མཐའ་དང་སྤྲོས་པའི་རྣམ་པ་གང་ཅིར་ཡང་མི་རྟོག་ཀྱང་། གནས་ལུགས་དམིགས་སུ་མེད་པའི་དོན་དེ་ཐེ་ཚོམ་གྱི་རབ་རིབ་མེད་པའི་སོ་སོ་རང་རིག་པའི་ཡེ་ཤེས་ཀྱི་སྣང་བ་ཁོང་ནས་ཤར་བ་ལ་རྣམ་པར་མི་རྟོག་པའི་ཡེ་ཤེས་ཉིད་དུ་ཤེས་པར་བྱའོ། །

There is also the case of *things* that are nonconceptual *in their* very *composition.* These include forms and any other object as well as the sensory faculties of the eye and so on, which are material and therefore nonconceptual in their very makeup, without their being nonconceptual wisdom because of that.

Predetermination, whereby one were to think, "Now I will not form any concept whatsoever," would not be nonconceptual either, because to engage in predetermination in the sense of explicitly and consciously thinking, "I will not form a concept," would be a case of deliberate mental grasping which itself would involve entertaining attributes[53] and would therefore not be nonconceptual.

These *are the five* areas whose nature is such that the term "nonconceptual" is applied, *the* unqualified *exclusion of which* reveals *the concrete characteristic*[54] of nonconceptual original wisdom.

Hence, nonconceptual original wisdom itself should be understood to be that which does not conceptualize extremes or think in terms of any aspect of conceptual elaborations whatsoever. Not only that, it should also be understood to be the non-referential abiding nature itself which, without any distorting filter[55] of doubt, primordially knows itself through the light of intimate, detailed selfawareness shining from within.

གསུམ་པ།

ཁྱད་པར་ཡོངས་སུ་ཤེས་པ་ནི།
རྣམ་པར་མི་རྟོག་པ་ཉིད་དང་།
ཉེ་ཚེ་བ་ནི་མ་ཡིན་དང་།
གནས་མེད་པ་དང་གཏན་དུ་དང་།
གོང་ན་མེད་པའི་རྣམ་པ་སྟེ།
ཁྱད་པར་རྣམ་པ་ལྔ་ཡིན་ནོ།

ཁྱད་པར་ཡོངས་སུ་ཤེས་པ་ནི། འཁོར་འདས་ལ་བླང་དོར་དུ་རྣམ་པར་མི་རྟོག་པ་ཉིད་དང་། སྤངས་རྟོགས་ཉེ་ཚེ་བ་ནི་མ་ཡིན་པར་ཡོངས་སུ་རྫོགས་པ་དང་། སྲིད་པ་དང་ཞི་བའི་མཐའ་གང་ལའང་གནས་པ་མེད་པ་དང་། ཆོས་ཀྱི་སྐུ་རྟག་པའི་ངོ་བོས་གཞན་དོན་དུ་འཁོར་བ་སྲིད་དུ་བཞུགས་པས་གཏན་དུ་བ་ཡིན་པ་དང་། འདིའི་གོང་ན་གཞན་མེད་པའི་ཕྱིར་ཐམས་ཅད་ཀྱི་མཆོག་བླ་ན་མེད་པའི་རྣམ་པ་སྟེ། འདི་དག་ནི་ཉན་རང་ལས་ཁྱད་པར་འཕགས་པའི་ཚུལ་རྣམ་པ་ལྔ་ཡིན་ཏེ། ཉན་རང་དག་ནི་འཁོར་འདས་སུ་རྣམ་པར་རྟོག་པ་སོགས་ཀྱིས་ཁྱད་པར་འདི་དག་དང་མི་ལྡན་པ་ཡིན་ནོ། །

(iii) Fully understanding the distinctive marks

Completely understanding its marks refers
To its being free of conceptualization as such,
To the fact that it is not transitional,
To its not remaining while being there all along,
And its hallmark of being completely unexcelled;
These make up its five distinctive marks.

Completely understanding this wisdom's special *marks refers to* understanding the fact of *its being free of* the *conceptualization as such* of a rejection of samsara and an adoption of nirvana; *the fact that it is not* a *transitional* relinquishment and realization but the full completion of these; *its not remaining* in either extreme of conditioned existence or pacification, *while being* present *all along* because it persists in samsaric existence for the sake of others by virtue of the dharmakaya, which is permanent in essence; *its hallmark of being* unsurpassed, supreme over all, in that it is *completely unexcelled* by anything else. *These make up* the *five distinctive marks* of *its* superiority over the attainments of the Shravakas and Pratyekabuddhas, since they, in conceptualizing a samsara and nirvana and so on, fall short of these features.

བཞི་པ།

ཐ་མ་ལས་ཡོངས་ཤེས་པ་ནི།
རྣམ་རྟོག་རིང་དུ་བྱེད་པ་དང་།
བླ་ན་མེད་པའི་བདེ་སྟེར་དང་།
ཉོན་མོངས་པ་དང་ཤེས་བྱ་ཡི།
སྒྲིབ་པ་བྲལ་བར་བྱེད་པ་སྟེ།
དེ་ཡི་རྗེས་ལས་ཐོབ་པ་ཡི།
ཡེ་ཤེས་ཤེས་བྱའི་རྣམ་པ་ནི།
ཐམས་ཅད་ལ་ནི་འཇུག་པ་དང་།
སངས་རྒྱས་ཞིང་ནི་སྦྱོང་བ་དང་།
སེམས་ཅན་ཡོངས་སུ་སྨིན་བྱེད་དང་།
རྣམ་པ་ཐམས་ཅད་མཁྱེན་པ་ཉིད།
གཏོང་ཅིང་སྟེར་བར་བྱེད་པ་སྟེ།
རྣམ་ལྔ་ལས་ཀྱི་ཁྱད་པར་རོ།

ཡོངས་སུ་ཤེས་པ་རྣམ་པ་བཞི་ཡོད་པའི་ཐ་མ་དེའི་བྱེད་ལས་ཡོངས་སུ་ཤེས་པ་ནི། རྣམ་པར་རྟོག་པ་མངོན་དུ་རྒྱུ་རིང་དུ་བྱེད་པ་སྟེ། དེ་ནི་དེའི་ཀུན་ནས་ལྡང་བ་བཅོམ་པའི་ཕྱིར་སྐྱེས་བུ་བྱེད་པའི་འབྲས་བུ་དང་། བླ་ན་མེད་པའི་བདག་ཉིད་ཟག་མེད་ཀྱི་བདེ་བ་སྟེར་བར་བྱེད་པ་ནི་ཆོས་ཀུན་ཕྱིན་ཅི་མ་ལོག་པར་རྟོགས་ཤིང་གཏན་དུ་རྟག་པའི་བདེ་བ་སྒྲུབ་

(iv) Fully understanding the five effects

The last, the full understanding of its effects,
Includes its lasting effect on conceptualization;
Its affording unsurpassable happiness;
Its effecting elimination of obscurations—
Afflicted emotions and cognitive obscurations;
The original wisdom attained in the wake of this
Provides the access to every aspect of knowledge;
It enables achieving attunement with buddha-fields
And thorough maturation of sentient beings,
And brings about revelation and transmission
Of knowledge which is complete in every aspect;
These five are the special features of the effects.

This point is *the last* of the four to be thoroughly comprehended, namely, *the full understanding of* the *effects*[56] of this wisdom. These *include*:

- *Its lasting effect on* the flux of *conceptualization*; this comprises "the result attained by a gifted being,"[57] because it affords the conquest over the conceptual process in its volatile state.
- *Its affording an* untainted *happiness unsurpassable* in character; this comprises "the subjective result,"[58] because it involves an unmistaken understanding of all phenomena and a lasting accomplishment of permanent happiness.

པའི་ཕྱིར་བདག་པོའི་འབྲས་བུ་དང་། ཉོན་མོངས་པ་དང་ཤེས་བྱ་ཡི་སྒྲིབ་པ་གཉིས་པོ་བྲལ་བར་བྱེད་པ་ནི། ཕྲ་རྒྱས་བག་ཆགས་དང་བཅས་པ་བཅོམ་པའི་ཕྱིར་བྲལ་བའི་འབྲས་བུ་དང་། མི་རྟོག་པའི་ཡེ་ཤེས་དེ་ཡི་རྗེས་ལས་ཐོབ་པའི་ཆོས་རྣམས་ཀྱི་རང་མཚན་ཕྱིན་ཅི་མ་ལོག་པར་རྟོགས་པའི་ཡེ་ཤེས་ཀྱིས་ཤེས་བྱའི་རྣམ་པ་ནི་ཐམས་ཅད་པ་ནི་གཟིགས་པ་ཐོགས་པ་མེད་པར་འཇུག་པ་རྒྱུ་མཐུན་པའི་འབྲས་བུ་དང་སངས་རྒྱས་ཀྱི་ཞིང་ནི་ཡོངས་སུ་སྦྱོང་བ་དང་། སེམས་ཅན་ཡོངས་སུ་སྨིན་པར་བྱེད་དང་། རྣམ་པ་ཐམས་ཅད་མཁྱེན་པ་ཉིད་ཀྱི་ཆོས་རང་གི་རྒྱུད་ལ་གཏོད་ཅིང་ཡོངས་སུ་རྫོགས་པར་བྱེད་པ་དང་གཞན་ལ་སྟེར་བར་བྱེད་པ་དང་། དེ་གསུམ་གཅིག་ཏུ་བརྩིས་པ་རྣམ་སྨིན་གྱི་འབྲས་བུ་སྟེ། དེ་ལྟར་རྣམ་པ་ལྔ་ནི་རྣམ་པར་མི་རྟོག་པའི་ཡེ་ཤེས་ཀྱི་བྱེད་ལས་ཀྱི་ཁྱད་པར་རོ། །

བདུན་པ།

ཡིད་ལ་བྱེད་ལ་འཇུག་པ་ནི།
རྣམ་པར་མི་རྟོག་ཡེ་ཤེས་ལ།
འཇུག་པར་འདོད་པའི་གང་ཟག་ནི།
བྱང་ཆུབ་སེམས་དཔའ་གང་ཡིན་པ།
འདི་ལྟར་ཡིད་ལ་བྱེད་པ་སྟེ།

- *Its effecting elimination of obscurations,* both that of *afflicted emotions and* the *cognitive obscurations*; this comprises "the exclusive result," because it eliminates these in their maximal, minimal, and residual stages.
- *The original wisdom* of the post-meditative state, which unmistakenly understands the above-mentioned concrete-characteristic of all phenomena and which is *attained in the wake of this* nonconceptual wisdom of the meditative state of equipoise, *provides access to* an unhindered insight into *every aspect of knowledge*; this comprises "the correspondent result."
- It furthermore *enables* the *achieving* of complete *attunement with buddha-fields and* the *thorough maturation of sentient beings.* It *also brings about,* in one's own mindstream, the *revelation* and complete development of the qualities pertaining to the *knowledge which is complete in every aspect* as well as the *transmission* to others [of knowledge associated with the means of attaining these]; these three together constitute the fully ripened result.

These five are the special features of the effects induced by nonconceptual wisdom.

7) Mental cultivation

The introduction to mental cultivation:
For individuals wishing to cross the threshold
Into original nonconceptual wisdom,
For any bodhisattva, Awakening Hero,
Here is how to cultivate the mind.

དེ་བཞིན་ཉིད་ནི་མི་ཤེས་པས།
མི་བདེན་པར་ནི་ཡོངས་བརྟགས་པའི།
ས་བོན་ཐམས་ཅད་པ་ཞེས་པ།
མེད་པ་གཉིས་སུ་སྣང་བའི་རྒྱུ།
དེ་ལ་བརྟེན་པའི་ཐ་དད་རྒྱུ།
དེས་ནི་རྒྱུ་དང་འབྲས་བུར་བཅས།
སྣང་དུ་ཟིན་ཀྱང་མེད་པའོ།
དེ་སྣང་ཆོས་ཉིད་མི་སྣང་ཞིང་།
དེ་མི་སྣང་བས་ཆོས་ཉིད་སྣང་།
དེ་ལྟར་ཚུལ་བཞིན་ཡིད་བྱེད་ན།
བྱང་ཆུབ་སེམས་དཔའི་མི་རྟོག་པའི།
ཡེ་ཤེས་ལ་ནི་འཇུག་པའོ།
དེ་ལྟར་དམིགས་ལས་རྣམ་རིག་ཙམ།
དམིགས་ལས་དོན་རྣམས་མི་དམིགས་དང་།
དོན་རྣམས་མི་དམིགས་པ་ལས་ནི།
རྣམ་པར་རིག་ཙམ་མི་དམིགས་དང་།
དེ་མི་དམིགས་ལས་གཉིས་པོ་ནི།
ཁྱད་པར་མེད་པའི་དམིགས་ལ་འཇུག

By virtue of one's ignorance of suchness
The "store of all seeds" of what is unreal, mere invention,
Is the cause for two which do not exist to appear;
And, with that as the base, there are grounds for diversification,
Due to which the cause and effects as well,
In spite of appearing, still do not exist.
With that appearing, pure being does not appear;
Through that not appearing, pure being indeed appears.
Through such cultivation of mind, when properly done,
The Bodhisattva steps across the brink
Into original nonconceptual wisdom.
Through focusing thus, mere awareness is focused on,
Through which there **are** *no referents to focus on;*
Through there being no referents that could be focused on,
There is no such mere awareness to focus on;
Through that not existing on which to focus, the verge
Is crossed into focusing free of this twofold division;

དེ་གཉིས་ཁྱད་པར་མི་དམིགས་པ།
དེ་ནི་རྣམ་པར་མི་རྟོག་པའི།
ཡེ་ཤེས་ཡུལ་མེད་དམིགས་མེད་པ།
མཚན་མ་ཐམས་ཅད་མི་དམིགས་པས།
རབ་ཕྱེ་བ་ནི་ཡིན་ཕྱིར་རོ།

གནས་ཡོངས་སུ་གྱུར་པ་ཡིད་ལ་བྱེད་པའི་ཚུལ་ལ་ཇི་ལྟར་འཇུག་པ་ནི། རྟེན་རྣམ་པར་མི་རྟོག་པའི་ཡེ་ཤེས་དེ་ལ་ཚུལ་བཞིན་འཇུག་པར་འདོད་པའི་གང་ཟག་ནི། བྱང་ཆུབ་སེམས་དཔའ་གང་ཡིན་པ་དེས་འདི་ལྟར་ཡིད་ལ་བྱེད་པ་སྟེ། ཆོས་ཐམས་ཅད་ཀྱི་གནས་ལུགས་དེ་བཞིན་ཉིད་ནི་མི་ཤེས་པས་མི་བདེན་པར་ནི་གྱུར་དུ་ཟིན་ཀྱང་འཁྲུལ་པའི་བློའི་ངོར་ཡོངས་སུ་བརྟག་པའི་གཟུང་འཛིན་དུ་སྣང་བའི་ཆོས་རྣམས་ཀྱི་ས་བོན་ཐམས་ཅད་པ་ཀུན་གཞིའི་རྣམ་ཤེས་ཞེས་པ་གང་དེ་མེད་བཞིན་པ་གཟུང་འཛིན་གཉིས་སུ་སྣང་བའི་རྒྱུ་ཡིན་ཏེ། ཐོག་མ་མེད་པའི་དུས་ཀྱི་སྦྱོར་བའི་བག་ཆགས་ཀྱིས་བགོས་པའི་རྣམ་ཤེས་ཀྱི་རྒྱུད་ཉིད་ལས་ཆོས་སྣ་ཚོགས་སུ་སྣང་བ་ནི་རྨི་ལམ་བཞིན་ནོ། །

ཀུན་གཞི་དེ་ལ་བརྟེན་པའི་འཇུག་ཤེས་གང་ཞིག་ཐ་དད་པའི་རྒྱུ་མཚན་ཅན་དེ། རང་ཡུལ་སོ་སོར་ངེས་པར་འཛིན་པ་ཅན་དུ་སྣང་བའང་འབྱུང་ངོ་། །

འདི་ལ་རྒྱུད་ཅེས་བྱས་པའང་སྣང་ངོ་། །

No split into two existing on which to focus,
This is original nonconceptual wisdom,
Since this is what is defined with the utmost precision
As that which involves no object, no focusing,
No attributes on which to focus at all.

The following is *the introduction* in*to* the procedure involved in the *mental cultivation* of complete transformation. It is designed *for individuals wishing* to find the way *to cross the threshold into original nonconceptual wisdom,* which serves as the support for this transformation. *For any*one who is a *Bodhisattva,* which means *Awakening Hero, here is how to cultivate the mind.*

By virtue of one's ignorance of suchness, the abiding nature of all phenomena, something forms which could be called "the all-inclusive base consciousness" or *the "store of all seeds" of what is* entirely *unreal,* namely, all phenomena, whose appearance as perceived and perceiver is the *mere invention* of a deluded intellect. That, in turn, serves as *the cause for* the *two,* perceived and perceiver, *which do not exist, to appear.* This appearance takes the form of the variety of phenomena manifesting from nowhere other than the stream of consciousness conditioned by habitual tendencies fabricated throughout beginningless time, like a dream.

With that all inclusive consciousness *as* the *base,* the necessary *grounds are* provided both *for* the *diversification* of consciousness into its various operative forms as well as for the appearance of the type of object specific to each type of consciousness in a nontransferable relation.[59] [In some texts] this [term "all-inclusive base consciousness"] also appears under the name "mind-stream."

ཡང་དག་མིན་པའི་ཀུན་རྟོག་གི་དབང་ལས་མེད་བཞིན་སྣང་བ་དེས་ནི་རྒྱུ་ཀུན་གཞི་དང་འབྲས་བུར་བཅས་པ་སྐྱེ་མཆེད་བདུན་ཡུལ་དང་བཅས་པའི་གཟུང་འཛིན་གཉིས་སྣང་གིས་བསྡུས་པའི་ཆོས་འདི་དག་འདི་ལྟ་བུར་འཁྲུལ་ངོར་སྣང་དུ་ཟིན་ཀྱང་། དོན་ལ་མེད་པ་སྒྱིག་རྒྱུ་ལ་སོགས་པ་བཞིན་དུ་རང་གི་ཡང་དག་པ་མིན་པའི་ཀུན་ཏུ་རྟོག་པ་ཙམ་དུ་གྲུབ་པའོ། །

གཟུང་འཛིན་གཉིས་པོ་དེ་སྣང་བས་ཆོས་ཉིད་མི་སྣང་ཞིང་། གཟུང་འཛིན་དེ་མི་སྣང་བས་ཆོས་ཉིད་སྣང་བ་ཡིན་ནོ་ཞེས། ཡང་དག་པ་མ་ཡིན་པའི་ཀུན་ཏུ་རྟོག་པ་དེའི་དབང་གིས་སེམས་ཅན་རྣམས་འཁོར་བར་འཁོར་ཞིང་ཆོས་ཉིད་མ་མཐོང་བ་ཡིན་པ་དེ་ལྟར་ཤེས་ཤིང་ཚུལ་བཞིན་ཡིད་ལ་བྱེད་ན་བྱང་ཆུབ་སེམས་དཔའ་དེ་ནི་རྣམ་པར་མི་རྟོག་པའི་ཡེ་ཤེས་ལ་ནི་ཐོག་མར་འཇུག་པ་ཡི་ཚུལ་དེ་ལྟ་བུ་ཡིན་ཏེ། རྣམ་པར་རྟོག་པའི་དབང་གིས་འཁོར་བར་སྣང་བ་ལས་རྒྱུ་གཞན་ཅི་ཡང་མེད་པས་ཀུན་ཉོན་ཕྱོགས་གཏན་ལ་དབབ་ཚུལ་ལ་གནད་འདི་ལས་ཟབ་པ་མེད་ཅིང་། གཉིས་སྣང་དེ་ནི་དེ་ལྟར་མ་གྲུབ་པས་ན་ཡང་དག་མིན་པའི་རྟོག་པ་ཙམ་དུ་ཤེས་ནས་དེ་ལ་དེར་ཞེན་སྤྲངས་ཏེ་རྣམ་པར་མི་རྟོག་པའི་ཡེ་ཤེས་ལ་འཇུག་པས་ནི་རྣམ་བྱང་ཕྱོགས་སྒྲུབ་པའི་ལམ་གྱི་གནད་ལའང་འདི་ཆེས་ཟབ་པའི་ཕྱིར་རོ། །

Due to it being that *which* does not exist that appears through the power of the mistaken conceptual process, *the cause*—the all-base consciousness—*and* its *effects*—the sevenfold collection together with the type of object specific to each type of consciousness—manifest *as well. Even though* in the eyes of delusion *these* do *appear* as such phenomena taking the form of dualistically appearing perceived and perceiver, they *do not exist* in reality but are merely one's own mistaken conceptual process,[60] as is the case with a mirage and so on.

With that dualism of perceived and perceiver *appearing, pure being does not appear; through that* percept and perceiver *not appearing, pure being indeed appears.*

This means that it is *through* knowing that sentient beings cycle in samsara without seeing pure being due to the mistaken conceptual process that *mental cultivation* can be *properly done, such* that *the Bodhisattva steps* for the first time *across the brink into original nonconceptual wisdom.* This is because (a) there is no more profound key to a firm understanding of afflictive factors than this insight into the appearance of samsara as having no other cause whatsoever than conceptuality, and (b) the most profound of all keys to the path on which refining factors are accomplished is the knowledge that dualistic appearance, in not existing as it seems, is merely a mistaken concept. This is how one abandons the assumption of its being what it appears to be. And this is how nonconceptual original wisdom is penetrated.

ཇི་སྐད་བཤད་པ་དེ་ལྟར་དམིགས་ཤིང་ཡིད་ལ་བྱེད་པ་གོམས་པ་ལས་ཆོས་ཐམས་ཅད་རྣམ་པར་རིག་པ་ཙམ་མམ་སེམས་ཙམ་དུ་དམིགས་པ་འབྱུང་ལ། དེ་ལས་ཕྱི་རོལ་གྱི་དོན་རྣམས་ཞེན་བྱར་མི་དམིགས་པ་ལ་འཇུག་པ་དང་། དེ་ལྟར་དོན་རྣམས་མི་དམིགས་པ་ལས་ནི། དེ་དང་དེར་འཛིན་པའི་རྣམ་པར་རིག་པ་ཙམ་དུའང་མི་དམིགས་པ་འབྱུང་བ་དང་། འཛིན་པ་དེ་མི་དམིགས་པ་ལས་གཟུང་འཛིན་གཉིས་པོ་ནི་ཁྱད་པར་བྱར་མེད་པ་གཉིས་སུ་མེད་པའི་དེ་བཞིན་ཉིད་བསམ་བརྗོད་ལས་འདས་པའི་དོན་དམིགས་པ་ལ་འཇུག་པ་འབྱུང་ལ། གཟུང་འཛིན་དེ་གཉིས་ཀྱི་ཁྱད་པར་དུ་གདོགས་པའི་ཆོས་གང་ཡང་མི་དམིགས་པ་དེ་ནི་རྣམ་པར་མི་རྟོག་པའི་ཡེ་ཤེས་ཞེས་བྱ་སྟེ་དེ་ལ་དམིགས་བྱའི་ཡུལ་ཅུང་ཟད་ཀྱང་མེད་པ་དང་། ཡུལ་ཅན་གྱིས་གང་དུ་དམིགས་པ་མེད་པ་དང་། དེའི་ཕྱིར་ན་གཟུང་བ་དང་འཛིན་པ་ཡོད་པ་དང་མེད་པ་ལ་སོགས་པའི་མཚན་མ་ཐམས་ཅད་ཅུང་ཟད་ཀྱང་མི་དམིགས་པས་རབ་ཏུ་ཕྱེ་བ་ནི་ཡིན་པའི་ཕྱིར་རྣམ་པར་རྟོག་པའི་ཕྱོགས་སུ་གཏོགས་པའི་རྒྱུ་མཚན་ཕྲ་མོ་ཡང་བཞག་རྒྱུ་མེད་པར་འགྱུར་རོ། །

Through habituation to a mental cultivation where *focusing* is practiced *thus*, i.e., as just explained, what will *be focused on* is all phenomena as being *mere* image-*awareness* or mind only. *Through this* the breakthrough is achieved in which *there are no* outer *referents,* as assumed, *on* which *to focus. Through there being no* such *referents that could be focused on,* it will follow that *there is* no perceiver of this and that, i.e., *no such "mere awareness" on* which *to focus. Through that* perceiver *not existing on which to focus, the verge is crossed into focusing* on reality, which is suchness transcending thought and expression and which is *free of* duality, in that there is no *twofold division* into perceived and perceiver. *This* having evolved, there are *no* phenomena whatsoever (meaning anything perceived and a perceiver of it as a result of a *split into* these *two*) *existing on which to focus.* This *is* what is called *"original nonconceptual wisdom," since this is what is defined with the utmost precision as that which involves no object* whatsoever serving as a focal referent, *no focusing* agent of any sort as an observer *and,* as a result, *no attributes* in any sense—such as the existence of perceived and perceiver, their nonexistence, and so on—*on which to focus at all.* Because of this, there are not even the subtlest grounds on which anything included under conceptual factors could be posited.

བརྒྱད་པ།

སྦྱོར་བས་ས་ལ་འཇུག་པ་ནི།
རྣམ་པ་བཞི་རུ་ཤེས་བྱ་སྟེ།
མོས་པས་རབ་ཏུ་སྦྱོར་བས་ནི།
མོས་པས་སྤྱོད་པའི་ས་ལ་སྟེ།
ངེས་པར་འབྱེད་པའི་གནས་སྐབས་སོ།
སོ་སོར་རབ་ཏུ་རྟོགས་པ་ཡི།
སྦྱོར་བས་ས་ནི་དང་པོ་སྟེ།
དེ་ཉིད་རིག་པའི་གནས་སྐབས་སོ།
བསྒོམ་པས་རབ་ཏུ་སྦྱོར་བས་ནི།
མ་དག་པ་ཡི་ས་དག་དང་།
དག་པའི་ས་ནི་གསུམ་པོ་སྟེ།
དེ་ནི་རྗེས་དྲན་གནས་སྐབས་སོ།
མཐར་ཕྱིན་པ་ལ་སྦྱོར་བས་ནི།
ལྷུན་གྱིས་གྲུབ་པར་སངས་རྒྱས་ཀྱི།
མཛད་པ་རྒྱུན་མི་འཆད་ཕྱིར་ཏེ།
དེ་ནི་དེ་ཡི་བདག་ཉིད་དུ།
ཉེ་བར་འགྲོ་བའི་གནས་སྐབས་སོ།

8) Application

The penetration of levels through application
Should be known to entail the following four steps:
Through intense application involving informed commitment,
The stage where training is done through informed commitment
Comprises the step of definitive verification.
To connect with superior, firsthand realization
Is the first of the levels, the stage the precise is encountered.
Through intense application employing meditation,
The impure levels followed by those which are pure
Are what comprise the stage of recollection.
Through application involving final perfection,
The spontaneous deeds of a buddha continually flow;
Hence, this is the stage of immersion into the core.

ཡེ་ཤེས་དེ་ཉམས་སུ་ལེན་པའམ་དེ་ལ་བརྩོན་ཅིང་སྦྱོར་བས་ས་དང་ལམ་གྱི་གནས་སྐབས་ཀྱི་སའམ་གཞི་སོ་སོ་ལ་འཇུག་པ་ནི་རྣམ་པ་བཞི་རུ་ཤེས་པར་བྱ་སྟེ། ཆོས་ཉིད་ཀྱི་དོན་མངོན་སུམ་དུ་མ་རྟོགས་ཀྱང་ཤེས་རབ་གསུམ་ལ་བརྟེན་ཏེ་མོས་པའི་སྒོ་ནས་དོན་དེ་ལ་རབ་ཏུ་སྦྱོར་བས་ནི། མོས་པས་སྤྱོད་པའི་ས་ལ་འཇུག་པ་སྟེ། ངེས་པར་འབྱེད་པའི་ཆ་དང་མཐུན་པ་སྦྱོར་ལམ་གྱི་གནས་སྐབས་སོ། །

ཆོས་ཉིད་ཀྱི་དོན་དོན་སྤྱི་ཙམ་དུ་མ་ཡིན་པར་སོ་སོར་རབ་ཏུ་རྟོགས་པ་ཡི་སྦྱོར་བས་ས་ནི་དང་པོ་ལ་འཇུག་པ་སྟེ་དེ་ཁོན་ཉིད་ལ་མངོན་སུམ་དུ་རིག་པའི་གནས་སྐབས་སོ། །

རྟོགས་ཟིན་དེ་ཉིད་ཡང་ཡང་བསྒོམས་པས་རབ་ཏུ་སྦྱོར་བས་ནི་ས་གཉིས་པ་ནས་བདུན་པའི་བར་གྱི་མ་དག་པ་ཡི་ས་དྲུག་ཏུ་གྲགས་པ་སྟེ་མཚན་མ་ཀུན་ཏུ་སྤྱོད་པ་དང་བཅས་པའི་གནས་སྐབས་དང་། མཚན་མ་ཀུན་ཏུ་སྤྱོད་པ་དེ་དག་པའི་ས་ནི་བརྒྱད་པ་ལ་སོགས་པ་གསུམ་པོ་ལ་འཇུག་སྟེ། ས་ལྷག་མ་དགུ་པོ་དེ་ནི་རྟོགས་ཟིན་གྱི་དོན་རྗེས་སུ་དྲན་པའི་གནས་སྐབས་སོ། །

The penetration of the distinctive plateaus or levels of development comprising the graded progression of *the* paths and *levels* occurs *through* practicing original wisdom, that is to say, through the *application* and effort expended in actually experiencing it. This *should be known to include the following four steps.*

There is a *stage* where the reality of pure being has not yet been realized directly but *where training is done through informed commitment.* This stage is entered *through intense application* to that reality and *involves* an *informed commitment* which is based on the three types of knowledge.[61] This *comprises the step* associated with the path of application, which is an approximation *of definitive verification.*

Through connecting with superior realization of the reality of pure being in an immediate, *firsthand* fashion, not through having a mere abstract idea[62] of it, *the* bhumis or *levels* of a realized Bodhisattva are entered, *the first of* which *is the stage* where *the precise* nature *is* directly *encountered.*

Through intense application employing repeated *meditation* on the precise nature already realized, one enters what are known as "*the* six *impure levels.*" These include the second to the seventh and comprise the stage where attributes are still entertained. These are *followed by* the *three* levels, the eighth and onwards, *which are pure* in that they have been purified of this.[63] These last nine levels together *are what comprise the stage of recollection* of the reality already realized.

མཐར་ཕྱིན་པའི་ས་ལ་སྦྱོར་བས་ནི་འབད་རྩོལ་མེད་པར་ལྷུན་གྱིས་གྲུབ་པར་སངས་རྒྱས་ཀྱི་མཛད་པ་ནམ་མཁའ་དང་སེམས་ཅན་གྱི་མཐའ་ཇི་སྲིད་དུ་རྒྱུན་མི་འཆད་པར་འཇུག་པའི་ཕྱིར་རོ། སྦྱོར་བ་དེ་ནི་སྒྲིབ་གཉིས་སྤྲངས་པའི་ཆོས་ཉིད་དེ་ཡི་བདག་ཉིད་དུ་ཉེ་བར་སོན་པའམ་འགྲོ་བའི་གནས་སྐབས་ཏེ་དབྱིངས་དང་གཉིས་སུ་མེད་པ་འགྱུར་མེད་ཀྱི་ཡེ་ཤེས་སོ། །

དགུ་པ།

ཉེས་དམིགས་དག་ལ་འཇུག་པ་ནི།

གནས་ཡོངས་གྱུར་པ་མེད་པ་ཡི།

ཉེས་དམིགས་བཞི་སྟེ་ཉོན་མོངས་པ།

མི་འཇུག་རྟེན་མེད་ཉེས་པ་དང་།

ལམ་འཇུག་རྟེན་མེད་ཉེས་པ་དང་།

མྱ་ངན་འདས་པའི་གང་ཟག་རྣམས།

གདགས་པའི་གཞི་མེད་ཉེས་པ་དང་།

བྱང་ཆུབ་གསུམ་གྱི་ཁྱད་པར་དག

གདགས་པའི་གཞི་མེད་ཉེས་པའོ།

ཉེས་དམིགས་དག་ལ་འཇུག་པ་ནི་གང་ཞེ་ན། གནས་ཡོངས་སུ་གྱུར་པ་མེད་པ་ཡི་ཉེས་དམིགས་བཞི་སྟེ་ཉོན་མོངས་པ་སྤྲངས་ཟིན་པ་རྣམས་སླར་ཡང་རྒྱུད་དེར་མི་འཇུག་པའི་རྟེན་མེད་པའི་ཉེས་པ་དང་། གཉེན་པོ་ལམ་ཉིད་རྒྱུད་དེ་ལ་འཇུག་པའི་རྟེན་མེད་པའི་ཉེས

Through application involving the level of *final perfection,* one enters into *the spontaneous* and effortless *deeds of a buddha*, which flow *without interruption* for as long as there are beings throughout the reaches of space. *Hence, this* form of application, which is purified of the two obscurations, *is the stage of immersion into the core* of pure being, the unchanging wisdom which is not something distinct from the expanse.

9) The disadvantages

The introduction to disadvantages
Includes the four that would follow as a result
Of there being no transformation; namely, the flaw
That preventing afflictions' entry would lack a support;
The flaw of the path's introduction lacking support;
The flaw of there being no basis of imputation
For speaking of individuals reaching nirvana;
As well as the flaw of no basis of imputation
For distinctions between three forms of enlightenment.

For those who ask what *the introduction to* the *disadvantages* involves, it *includes the four that would follow as a* result *of there being no* such thing as a *transformation* undergone. These are as follows:

- *The flaw that preventing afflictions'* re-*entry* into the mindstream after its already having been purged of them *would lack a support*ing ground
- T*he flaw of the path's*, i.e., the remedy's, *introduction* into the mindstream *lacking* a *support*ing ground

པ་དང་། མྱ་ངན་ལས་འདས་པའི་གང་ཟག་རྣམས་སུ་གདགས་པའི་གཞི་མེད་པའི་ཉེས་པ་དང་། ཉན་རང་ཐེག་ཆེན་གྱི་མཐར་འབྲས་བྱང་ཆུབ་གསུམ་གྱི་ཁྱད་པར་དག་གདགས་པའི་གཞི་མེད་པའི་ཉེས་པ་དང་བཞིར་འགྱུར་བ་ཤེས་པར་བྱའོ། །

དེ་ཡང་དེའི་གོ་བའི་གནད་རྒྱས་པར་བཤད་ན། ལམ་གྱིས་སྤང་བྱ་སྤང་ཞིང་རྟོགས་པ་ཐོབ་པའི་གནས་གྱུར་དེ་གལ་ཏེ་མེད་ན། ཉོན་མོངས་པ་སྤངས་ཟིན་པ་རྣམས་སླར་རྒྱུད་དེ་ལ་མི་འཇུག་པའི་རྟེན་མེད་པའི་ཉེས་པ་ཡོད་དེ། དཔེར་ན་མཐོང་སྤང་སྤངས་པའི་རྒྱུད་ལ་སླར་སྤང་བྱ་དེ་མི་འབྱུང་བ་ནི་བྱང་སེམས་དེའི་རྒྱུད་ཡོངས་སུ་གྱུར་པའི་གནས་གྱུར་ཐོབ་པའི་ཕྱིར་རྟེན་དེ་ལ་དེ་འཇུག་པའི་སྐབས་མེད་པ་ཡིན་གྱི་གཞན་དུ་སྒྲིབ་པ་ལན་གཅིག་སྤངས་སུ་ཟིན་ཀྱང་སེམས་ཀྱི་རྒྱུད་གནས་མ་གྱུར་ན་སླར་ཡང་སྔར་བཞིན་སྐྱེ་བར་འགྱུར་རོ། །

དེ་བཞིན་དུ་སངས་རྒྱས་ཀྱི་སའི་བར་དུ་ཤེས་པར་བྱ་སྟེ། རྒྱུད་གང་ཞིག་གནས་མ་གྱུར་པའི་ཚེ་སྤང་བྱ་དེ་དང་དེ་འཇུག་པའི་རྟེན་དུ་གྱུར་ལ། གནས་གྱུར་པའི་ཚེ་སྤང་བྱ་དེ་དག་མི་འཇུག་པའི་རྟེན་དུ་གྱུར་པ་ནི་གནས་གྱུར་པ་ཡོད་པའི་དབང་གིས་ཡིན་ནོ། །

ས་བོན་མེས་བསྲེགས་པ་བཞིན་དུ་སྤང་བྱའི་ས་བོན་བཅོམ་པ་ན་སླར་མི་སྐྱེ་བ་ཙམ་ཡིན་གྱི་གནས་གྱུར་ཞེས་པ་མེད་ཀྱང་ཅི་འགལ་སྙམ་ན། སྤང་བྱའི་ས་བོན་བཅོམ་པ་ཡིན་མོད་ཀྱི་དེ་ཡང་རྒྱུད་གང་གི་ཁྱད་པར་དུ་བྱས་ནས་འཇོག་དགོས་ཀྱི་ཁྱད་པར་མེད་པ་ལ་མི་རུང་

- *The flaw of there being no basis of imputation for speaking of individuals reaching nirvana*
- *The flaw of* there being *no basis of imputation for* the *distinctions* that are made *between* the *three forms of enlightenment* constituting the ultimate fruition for Shravakas, Pratyekabuddhas and Mahayana practitioners.

As a key to the understanding of this, the following expanded explanation is provided.

If there were no such thing as a transformation, achieved through the practice of the path whereby the factors to be given up are surrendered and realization is accomplished, the flaw would ensue of there being no sure way of preventing a recurrence in the mindstream of afflictions already eliminated. Take, for example, the factors eliminated by the path of seeing. Such factors, once eliminated, do not recur in the mindstream, because the mind continuum of the Bodhisattva has undergone a complete transformation such that the occasion or basis for such factors to occur is no longer present. Otherwise, without this transformation of the mind continuum, obscurations once eliminated could recur as before.

And that holds true all the way up to and including the level of buddhahood. As long as a given mindstream has not undergone transformation, it serves as a support, or container, for factors requiring elimination; as soon as it has undergone transformation, it becomes a support for such factors not recurring due to the metamorphosis that has taken place.

The objection could be raised, "What would be the problem in saying that, once the seeds in the form of factors to be eliminated had been destroyed, they would simply not regenerate—as with seeds consumed by fire—in which case, there would be no talk of a 'transformation'."

In reply, the seeds in the form of factors to be eliminated would indeed have been destroyed; nevertheless, this must necessarily be posited in relation to a specific mindstream.

སྟེ་གཉེན་པོའི་ཡེ་ཤེས་རྒྱུད་ལ་བསྐྱེད་པའི་རྒྱུད་ཀྱི་ཁྱད་པར་ལ་ལར་ཟག་པ་ཟད་པ་ཞེས་དམིགས་ཕྱེ་སྟེ་མ་བསྟན་པར་ས་བོན་བཅོམ་ཚུལ་ཀྱང་མི་ཤེས་པའི་ཕྱིར་རོ། །

དེ་ལྟ་ན་སྤང་བྱའི་ས་བོན་ཟད་པའི་རྒྱུད་དེ་ལ་སྔར་ལས་གནས་གྱུར་པའི་ཁྱད་པར་དེས་སླར་མི་སྐྱེ་བ་ཡིན་གྱི་རྒྱུད་རྒྱུན་ཆད་ནས་རྟེན་མེད་པར་སོང་བ་ལྟ་བུ་ནི་མ་ཡིན་པའི་ཕྱིར་རྒྱུད་ཀྱི་ཁྱད་པར་ལ་ལར་ཟག་པ་རྣམས་སྐྱེ་བ་དང་ལ་ལར་མི་སྐྱེ་བ་འདི་གནས་གྱུར་མ་ཐོབ་པ་དང་ཐོབ་པའི་དབང་གིས་ཏེ་རབ་རིབ་མེད་པའི་མིག་ལ་སྐྲ་ཤད་ཀྱི་སྣང་བ་སྐབས་མི་མཐོང་བ་བཞིན་ནོ། །

ཡང་གནས་ཡོངས་སུ་གྱུར་པ་མེད་ན་སྤང་བྱའི་གཉེན་པོ་ལམ་འཇུག་པའི་རྟེན་མེད་པའི་ཉེས་པ་ཡོད་པར་འགྱུར་ཏེ། གང་ཟག་འདི་ནི་མཐོང་ལམ་པའོ་འདི་ནི་ས་གཉིས་པའོ་ཞེས་སོགས་རྒྱུད་ཀྱི་ཁྱད་པར་ལ་ལམ་གོང་མ་གོང་མ་དག་འཇུག་པའི་རྟེན་ནི་གནས་གྱུར་སྔ་མ་སྔ་མ་ཡིན་ཏེ་སྔ་མ་སྔ་མ་མེད་པར་ཕྱི་མ་ཕྱི་མ་འབྱུང་མི་སྲིད་པའི་ཕྱིར་ཏེ། ས་བོན་མྱུ་གུར་གནས་གྱུར་པ་མེད་ན་སྡོང་བུ་སོགས་འབྱུང་བ་སྐབས་མི་ཐོབ་པ་བཞིན་ནོ། །

གནས་གྱུར་དེ་དང་དེ་ལའང་ལམ་དེ་དང་དེའི་ཐ་སྙད་དང་དོན་གཉིས་ཀ་འཇུག་སྟེ། སངས་རྒྱས་པའི་ས་ལ་མི་སློབ་ལམ་ཞེས་པ་བཞིན་ནོ། །

ཡང་གནས་ཡོངས་སུ་གྱུར་པ་མེད་ན་མྱང་འདས་སུ་གདགས་པའི་གཞི་མེད་པའི་ཉེས་པ་ཡོད་དེ། དཔེར་ན་ཟག་པ་དང་བཅས་པའི་ཕུང་པོའི་རྒྱུན་ལ་གདགས་གཞི་བྱས་ཏེ་འདི་

Not to specify it thus would be indefensible for the following reason. If it had not been taught that any case of termination of the tainted condition is precisely determined in relation to some specific mindstream in which the remedial wisdom has been put into practice, there would be no way of knowing how such seeds are destroyed.

This being so, it is because of the difference represented by the transformation of the previous state of the mindstream that the seeds of factors to be purged, once eliminated, do not recur. It is not that the supporting ground, which is the mindstream, disappears, as it were, due to an interruption of its continuity. It is, therefore, due to the lack of attainment of this transformation or its attainment that there are some specific mindstreams in which taint occurs and others in which it does not, just as no occasion presents itself for the appearance of strands of hair for an eye in which cataracts have been removed.

The next flaw would be that, if no transformation occurred, there would be no basis for entering a path whereby factors requiring elimination could be remedied. The underlying basis for entering progressively higher paths on the part of specific mindstreams, such that one individual can be said to be on the path of vision, another on the second level and so on, is the prior transformation undergone in each case, since, without the prior, the latter could not possibly occur—just as, without the transformation of the seed into the sprout, there would be no occasion for the development of a stalk and so on. It is in relation to a specific transformation that a specific path is entered and its contents and conventions apply, as is the case with the level of buddhahood, which is given the name "the path of no more learning."

Regarding the next, if no transformation had been undergone, the flaw of there being no basis of imputation for the term "nirvana" would apply. This could be illustrated as follows. Just as the term "samsaric individual" has

ནི་གང་ཟག་འཁོར་བ་པའོ་ཞེས་གདགས་པ་བཞིན་དུ། ཟག་པ་མེད་པར་གནས་གྱུར་པ་དེ་ཉིད་ལ་གདགས་གཞིར་བྱས་ཏེ་འདི་ནི་མྱ་ངན་འདས་པའི་གང་ཟག་གོ་ཞེས་གདགས་ཀྱི་གནས་གྱུར་མེད་པར་སེམས་ལ་སོགས་པའི་ཕུང་པོའི་རྒྱུན་ཙམ་ལ་ནི་མྱ་ངན་ལས་འདས་པའི་གང་ཟག་ཏུ་གདགས་པའི་གཞི་མེད་པར་འགྱུར་ཏེ་སྔར་གནས་མ་གྱུར་པའི་གནས་སྐབས་བཞིན་ནོ། །

གཞན་ཡང་ཉན་རང་རང་ལམ་ན་འདོད་པ་ལྟར་གྱི་ཕུང་པོ་ལྷག་མ་མེད་པའི་དབྱིངས་སུ་མྱ་ངན་ལས་འདས་པའི་གང་ཟག་རྣམས་ལའང་མྱ་ངན་ལས་འདས་པ་ཞེས་གདགས་པའི་གཞི་མེད་པར་འགྱུར་ཏེ་གནས་གྱུར་མེད་ན་དེ་ལྟར་བཏགས་པ་དེ་རི་བོང་གི་རྭའི་མིང་བཞིན་གཞི་མེད་པའི་མིང་དུ་འགྱུར་རོ། །

དེ་ལ་གཞི་མེད་ཀྱང་མི་རུང་བ་ཅི་ཡོད་དེ་སྔར་གྱི་ཕུང་པོ་འགག་པ་ཙམ་ལ་མྱང་འདས་སུ་འདོགས་ཏེ་ནད་ཞི་བ་ལ་ནད་མེད་དོ་ཞེས་བརྗོད་པ་བཞིན་ནོ་སྙམ་ན། སྔར་གྱི་ཕུང་པོ་རྒྱུན་ཆད་ཅིང་སླར་མི་སྐྱེ་བའི་ངེས་པ་ཡོད་ན་ནི་དེ་ཉིད་དེའི་གནས་གྱུར་ཡིན་པས་གནས་གྱུར་ཀྱང་ཡོད་པར་འགྱུར་ཏེ། གང་ཟག་འདི་ནི་མྱ་ངན་ལས་འདས་སོ། །སླར་འཁོར་བར་མི་ལྡང་ངོ་ཞེས་པའི་རྟེན་དང་གདགས་གཞི་གཉིས་ཀ་གནས་གྱུར་དེ་ཡིན་པས་དེ་མེད་པར་ཁས་བླང་དུ་མི་བཏུབ་ལ། གལ་ཏེ་གནས་གྱུར་མེད་པར་ཁས་བླངས་

as its basis of imputation the continuity of a set of tainted aggregates, the imputation of the term "nirvanic individual" has nothing else as its base of imputation than the metamorphosis in which taint has disappeared. Without that transformation, there would be no other basis for the term "nirvanic individual" than the continuity of aggregates, mental and otherwise, and these would be the same as they had been before, where no transformation had taken place.

Furthermore, there would be no basis with respect to which the term "nirvana" could be employed in the case of those individuals who had attained the nirvana of "the expanse without remainder of aggregates[64]" as this is asserted by the Shravakas and Pratyekabuddhas in the context of their own paths. Without a transformation, such an imputation would be a name without a basis, like the name "rabbit horns."

The objection could be raised, "Even though there would be no basis in the mentioned context, what would be wrong with that? One could impute the term 'nirvana' to the mere cessation of the prior aggregates, just as one would apply the term 'not infirm' to a case in which an illness has been eliminated."

In reply, if it is an unequivocal case of the continuity of prior aggregates being interrupted without their recurrence, since precisely that would constitute a transformation of these, a metamorphosis would in any case have been undergone, since it is this transformation which would provide both the grounds for saying, "Samsara will be fallen into no more," as well as the basis for the name "an individual who has attained nirvana." One could not make such statements without it. If one were to make such claims without

ན་ཕུང་པོ་རྒྱུན་ཆད་པ་དང་སླར་མི་སྐྱེ་བ་ཡང་མེད་པར་འགྱུར་ཏེ་དེའི་རྟེན་དང་གདགས་གཞི་གཉིས་ཀ་མེད་པའི་ཕྱིར་རོ། །

གལ་ཏེ་ཐེག་པ་ཆེན་པོའི་ལམ་གྱིས་ཟག་བཅས་ཀྱི་ཕུང་པོ་ལྷག་མ་མེད་པའི་དབྱིངས་སུ་མྱ་ངན་ལས་འདས་ཀྱང་ཟག་མེད་ཀྱི་སྐུ་དང་ཡེ་ཤེས་རྒྱུན་མི་འཆད་པའི་ཕྱིར་འདས་ལྟར་ན་དེ་ནི་གནས་ཡོངས་སུ་གྱུར་པའི་བདག་ཉིད་ཡིན་པ་སྨོས་མ་དགོས་སོ། །

ཡང་ཐེག་པ་གསུམ་གྱི་འབྲས་བུ་བྱང་ཆུབ་ཅེས་ཁྱད་པར་མི་འདྲ་བ་གསུམ་དུ་འཇོག་པ་དེ་ནི་གནས་གྱུར་གྱི་ཁྱད་པར་མི་འདྲ་བ་ལས་ཡིན་ཏེ། སྒྲིབ་པ་ཕྱོགས་རེ་བ་དང་མཐའ་དག་དག་པའི་ཁྱད་པར་གྱིས་དེ་ལྟར་འཇོག་དགོས་པ་ཡིན་ཀྱང་། གནས་ཡོངས་སུ་གྱུར་བ་ཉིད་མེད་ན་བྱང་ཆུབ་གསུམ་གྱི་ཁྱད་པར་འདི་དང་འདི་ཞེས་གདགས་པའི་གཞི་མེད་པར་འགྱུར་ཏེ་ཕུང་པོ་ལྷག་མ་མེད་པའི་དབྱིངས་སུ་མྱ་ངན་ལས་འདས་པའི་ཚེ་བྱང་ཆུབ་གསུམ་གྱི་ཁྱད་པར་གང་ལ་འདོགས་པའི་གཞི་མེད་པར་འགྱུར་བས་ནི། དེ་དག་གི་སྤྱང་རྟོགས་ཀྱི་ཡོན་ཏན་ཆེ་ཆུང་སོགས་བཤད་པ་རྣམས་མོ་གཤམ་གྱི་བུའི་མཛེས་མི་མཛེས་བཤད་པ་བཞིན་དུ་དོན་མེད་པར་འགྱུར་རོ། །

འདི་དག་རྒྱ་བོད་ཀྱི་འགྲེལ་བ་སྔ་མ་རྣམས་སུ་ཞིབ་པར་མ་གསུངས་པས་འདིར་རྒྱས་པར་བཤད་པ་ལ་བློ་ལྡན་རྣམས་དགྱེས་པར་མཛོད་ཅིག །

transformation taking place, there would be no stopping the continuity of the skandhas and no way to prevent their recurrence, since there would be neither an underlying support for that nor a basis with reference to which such terms could be employed.

That being so [in the case of nirvana as defined in the Shravaka- and Pratyekabuddha paths], there is no need to mention that the nirvana attained through the Mahayana path—which is not only a transcendence of misery in the expanse of freedom from any remainder of tainted aggregates but is also a nirvana in which there is an uninterrupted continuity of untainted kayas and wisdom—is of the nature of a transformation.

Regarding the last case, the positing of different types of enlightenment as the result of the three vehicles, these are necessarily posited with respect to the distinct differences in the transformation undergone in each case, and this depends on whether the purification of obscurations has been partial or complete. Without a specific transformation in each case, there would be no basis for differentiating between three specific types of enlightenment, and, when someone achieved the nirvana which is the expanse free of remainder of aggregates, there would be no basis for saying which of the three types of enlightenment was attained. So, explanations comparing their qualities of relinquishment and realization in terms of greater and lesser and so on would be as meaningless as comparing the sons of a barren woman in terms of their being handsome or not.

Since these points have not been addressed in any detail in earlier commentaries, either in India or Tibet, we have discussed them extensively here. May those of fine judgment find this presentation satisfactory.

བཅུ་པ་ནི།

བཟློག་ནས་ཕན་ཡོན་འཇུག་པ་ནི།
རྣམ་པ་བཞི་རུ་ཤེས་པར་བྱའོ།

བཤད་མ་ཐག་པ་གནས་ཡོངས་སུ་གྱུར་པ་མེད་པའི་ཉེས་པ་བཞི་ལས་བཟློག་ནས་དེ་ཡོད་པ་ལ་ཕན་ཡོན་ཡོད་པའི་ཚུལ་ལ་འཇུག་པ་ནི་རྣམ་པ་བཞི་རུ་སྔ་མའི་དོན་གྱིས་ཤེས་པར་བྱ་སྟེ། རྒྱུད་ཀྱི་ཁྱད་པར་གང་ཞིག་རྒྱུན་ཆད་པ་མེད་པར་ཡོད་ཀྱང་སྔ་མ་ལས་གནས་ཡོངས་སུ་གྱུར་པའི་བདག་ཉིད་དུ་གནས་པ་ཡོད་ན། ཉོན་མོངས་པ་རྣམས་གཏན་དུ་མི་འཇུག་པར་བྱེད་པའི་རྟེན་ཡོད་པ་དང་། ལམ་འཇུག་པའི་རྟེན་ཡོད་པ་དང་། མྱ་ངན་ལས་འདས་པར་གདགས་པའི་གཞི་ཡོད་པ་དང་། ཐེག་པ་གསུམ་གྱིས་རྣམ་གྲོལ་བྱང་ཆུབ་གསུམ་གྱི་ཁྱད་པར་ཕྱེས་ཏེ་གདགས་པའི་གཞི་ཡོད་པར་འགྱུར་ཏེ་དེ་ལྟར་ན་གནས་ཡོངས་སུ་གྱུར་པའི་ཡེ་ཤེས་དེ་ནི་རྣམ་པར་གྲོལ་བའི་བྱང་ཆུབ་དང་མྱ་ངན་ལས་འདས་པའི་གདགས་གཞི་ཡོན་ཏན་མི་ཟད་པའི་འབྱུང་གནས་ནམ་མཁའ་ཇི་སྲིད་དུ་སེམས་ཅན་མ་ལུས་པའི་གནས་སྐབས་དང་མཐར་ཐུག་གི་དོན་ཐམས་ཅད་ཡིད་བཞིན་རྗེས་སུ་སྒྲུབ་པའི་རྟེན་དམ་པ་ཡིན་པར་ཤེས་ནས་གང་ཟག་སྐལ་བ་དང་ལྡན་པ་རྣམས་ཀྱིས་དེ་སྒྲུབ་པ་ལ་འཇུག་པར་བྱའོ། །

10) The benefits

> *The introduction to the benefits*
> *Should be known to include these four, but in the reverse.*

The introduction to the sort of *benefits* that follow from there being a transformation *should be known to include these* same *four* points just explained *but in the reverse* sense of the four flaws that would follow if there were no transformation.

There is no discontinuation of a given, specific mindstream [when any of the three forms of nirvana is attained] but a transformation of the previous state. And this transformation is of an enduring nature. This being so, there is a reliable foundation for no recurrence of afflicted states, a ground that supports entering the paths, a basis for the imputation of the term "nirvana," and a basis for the imputation of specific distinctions between three types of liberating enlightenment gained by means of the three vehicles.

In this connection, it is the wisdom comprising complete transformation that provides the basis of imputation for terms like "nirvana" or "liberating enlightenment." It is the source of inexhaustible qualities, and the genuine support for the fulfillment, in accord with their wishes, of all temporary and ultimate aims of all sentient beings without exception as far as space extends. Those who know this are the fortunate ones. They should set about accomplishing it.

གསུམ་པ་ཇི་སྐད་བཤད་པའི་ཆོས་དང་ཆོས་ཉིད་དེའི་དོན་དཔེས་བསྟན་པའི་སྒོ་ནས་མཇུག་བསྡུ་བ་ནི།

མེད་པའི་ཆོས་རྣམས་སྣང་བའི་དཔེ།
སྒྱུ་མ་རྨི་ལམ་སོགས་པ་བཞིན།
གནས་ཡོངས་གྱུར་པ་དཔེར་བྱ་ན།
ནམ་མཁའ་གསེར་དང་ཆུ་སོགས་བཞིན།

ཡང་དག་པ་མ་ཡིན་པའི་ཀུན་ཏུ་རྟོག་པ་ཙམ་གྱི་དབང་གིས་སྣང་བ་འཁོར་བའི་ཆོས་རྣམས་ནི་མེད་པའི་ཆོས་ཞེས་བྱ་སྟེ་རང་གི་ངོ་བོ་མེད་བཞིན་དུ་སྣང་བའོ། །

དེ་རྣམས་མེད་བཞིན་དུ་ཡང་འཁྲུལ་ངོར་སྣང་བའི་དཔེ་ནི། ཇི་ལྟར་ན་སྒྱུ་མ་དང་རྨི་ལམ་དང་ཆུ་ཟླ་ལ་སོགས་པ་སྣང་ཡང་དེའི་ངོ་བོ་ཉིད་དུ་མེད་པ་བཞིན་ནོ། །

ཆོས་ཉིད་བཞིན་དུ་གནས་ཡོངས་སུ་གྱུར་པ་དཔེར་བྱ་ན་རང་བཞིན་གྱི་དག་པ་ནམ་མཁའ་དང་། གསེར་བཟང་པོ་དང་། ཆུ་ཁམས་དྭངས་བ་དང་། ཉི་མ་སྤྲིན་མེད་ལ་སོགས་པ་བཞིན་ཏེ། གནས་ཚུལ་ལ་ཆོས་ཐམས་ཅད་ཡེ་ནས་གཟུང་འཛིན་ལ་སོགས་པའི་དྲི་མ་མེད་པར་གནས་སུ་ཟིན་ཀྱང་། འཁྲུལ་པའི་དབང་གིས་གནས་ཚུལ་བསྒྲིབས་ཏེ་སྣང་ཚུལ་ལ་མ་དག་པ་ལྟར་སྣང་བའི་ཚེ་གནས་མ་གྱུར་པ་ཞེས་བྱ་ལ། དྲི་མ་དེ་ལམ་གྱིས་བསལ་བའི་སྟོབས་ཀྱིས་གནས་སྣང་རྣམ་པ་ཀུན་དུ་མཐུན་པའི་ཚེ་གནས་གྱུར་མཐར་ཐུག་

3 The concluding summary employing examples to illustrate the point

To show how phenomena not existing appear,
They are likened to dream and compared to illusion and so on;
To illustrate the total transformation,
To space it is likened, to gold and water and so on.

The examples used here clarify the sense of the above explanation of phenomena and pure being.

The phenomena of samsara, which appear by force of sheer mistaken conceptualization, are designated "*phenomena not existing*" and yet, while not existing with an essence of their own, they appear. *To show how* these could *appear* in the eyes of delusion without actually existing, *they are likened to illusion, dream*, the moon in the water, *and so on.* These are all cases in which there is an appearance but no essential component comprising it.

To illustrate the total transformation corresponding to pure being, *it is likened to space,* which is pure by nature; *to* pure *gold*; to *water,* which, in its basic constituent, is clean; to the sun, which is free of clouds, *and so on.*

Within fundamental being, no stain of perceived and perceiver or any other imperfection has ever been present from the very outset, but this basic state is obscured by delusion and that produces a seeming impurity in the realm of manifestation. For as long as this continues, "the untransformed condition" prevails. As soon as this stain has been removed through the path, being and manifestation stand reconciled in every respect and ultimate transformation has been attained.

པ་ཐོབ་པ་ཡིན་ཞིང༌། གནས་མ་གྱུར་པ་དང་གྱུར་པའི་སྐབས་ཐ་དད་པའི་འགྱུར་བ་དང་བཅས་པས་ན་ཆོས་ཉིད་ཡེ་ནས་དག་པའི་རང་བཞིན་དུ་མི་རུང་བ་དང༌། འགྱུར་བ་དང་བཅས་པར་མི་འགྱུར་རམ་ཞེ་ན་མི་འགྱུར་ཏེ་ཇི་ལྟར་ནམ་མཁའ་ཡེ་ནས་དག་པ་ལ་གློ་བུར་གྱི་ཁུག་རྣ་སོགས་དང་བཅས་པ་དང༌། གསེར་ལ་འདམ་དང༌། ཆུ་ལ་ས་རྫུལ་དང༌། ཉི་མ་སྤྲིན་སོགས་ཀྱིས་སྒྲིབ་པ་དང་བཅས་ཀྱང་དེ་དག་གི་ངོ་བོ་ལ་དེ་དང་དེས་བསླད་པ་མེད་ལ། དེ་དང་བྲལ་བའི་རང་བཞིན་མངོན་དུ་གྱུར་པ་ནའང་གསར་དུ་སྐྱེས་པ་མིན་པ་བཞིན་དུ་གློ་བུར་གྱི་དྲི་མ་དང་བྲལ་བའི་སྟོབས་ཀྱིས་གནས་གྱུར་ཐོབ་པའང་རང་བཞིན་གྱིས་འོད་གསལ་བའི་དོན་གློ་བུར་གྱི་དྲི་མས་བསྒྲིབས་ནས་སྔར་མི་སྣང་བ་ཕྱིས་ལམ་གྱི་སྟོབས་ལས་སྣང་བ་ཙམ་དུ་ཤེས་པར་བྱ་བ་ཡིན་ནོ། །

བཞི་པ་མཇུག་གི་དོན།

མཛད་བྱང་ནི།

ཆོས་དང་ཆོས་ཉིད་རྣམ་པར་འབྱེད་པའི་ཚིག་ལེའུར་བྱས་པ། མགོན་པོ་བྱམས་པས་མཛད་པ་རྫོགས་སོ། །

ཞེས་དང༌། འགྱུར་བྱང་ནི།

ཁ་ཆེའི་མཁན་པོ་མ་ཧཱ་ཛ་ན་དང༌། ཞ་མ་ལོ་ཙཱ་བ་དགེ་སློང་སེང་གེ་རྒྱལ་མཚན་གྱིས་བསྒྱུར་ཅིང་ཞུས་ཏེ་གཏན་ལ་ཕབ་པའོ། །

ཞེས་སོ། །

One might say, "There would be a difference between the phase where the transformation has not taken place and that where it has, so would it not be the case that pure being would not qualify as being the ever pure nature but would be changeable?"

No, it would not. Just as passing mist and so on can be present in the sky, which is primordially pure, without the sky being essentially affected by it, gold can be mixed with dross, water can be clouded by particles of dirt and the sun can be obscured by clouds without their being essentially affected.

Furthermore, even when the sky and so on, which are naturally free of polluting factors, become directly evident, they are not newly created. In the same way, when transformation has been attained by eliminating the superficial stains, this is merely a case of reality, which by its very nature is clear light, previously not appearing due to superficial stains, later appearing by virtue of the path.

IV The concluding statement

The fourth and concluding point includes the author's certification, which states,

> *The verses distinguishing phenomena and pure being composed by the guardian Maitreya are herewith concluded.*

and the translators' certification, which states,

> *The Kashmiri Khenpo Mahadzana and the Tibetan translator Shama Lotsawa Gelong Senge Gyaltsen collaborated in translating this [from Sanskrit into Tibetan] and in correcting their work, thus providing this finalized version.*

གཞུང་གི་དཀར་ཆག་ལྷན་དཀར་མ་སོགས་སུ་སྣ་འགྱུར་དུས་བསྒྱུར་བར་མ་གསུངས་ཀྱང་། ལོ་རྒྱུས་ཁ་ཅིག་ལས་བྱམས་ཆོས་སྡེ་ལྔ་ཀ་སྣ་འགྱུར་དུས་བསྒྱུར་ཞུས་གསུངས་ཏེ་དེ་དུས་མཁན་སློབ་སོགས་པཎ་ཆེན་དུ་མ་བཞུགས་ཤིང་རྒྱ་གར་དུ་བསྟན་པ་ཡོངས་རྫོགས་མཉམས་པའི་སྐབས་ཡིན་པས་བསྒྱུར་བར་གོར་མ་ཆག་གོ།

།རྒྱལ་ཚབ་སེམས་དཔའ་མཆོག་གི་བློ་གྲོས་ཀྱིས།
།རྒྱལ་བའི་དགོངས་དོན་ཚུལ་བཞིན་བཤད་པའི་གཞུང་།
།རྒྱལ་སྲས་རྣམས་ཀྱི་འཇུག་ངོགས་འདི་བཤད་དགེས།
།རྒྱལ་བསྟན་དྲི་མེད་ཕྱོགས་བཅུར་རྒྱས་གྱུར་ཅིག
།རྣམ་པར་མི་རྟོག་ཡེ་ཤེས་གངས་ཆེན་མཚོ།
།འཕགས་པའི་ཆོས་ཀྱི་རིན་ཆེན་འབྱུང་གནས་ལ།
།བདག་དང་འགྲོ་ཀུན་དགའ་བས་ལེགས་ཞུགས་ནས།
།རྫོགས་སྨིན་སྦྱོང་བ་མཐའ་རུ་ཕྱིན་པར་ཤོག །

ཅེས་པ་འདི་ན་སྔར་མེ་གླང་གི་ལོར་གདན་ས་འདིར་ཙམ་ལ་སྤྲུལ་པའི་སྐུ་རིན་པོ་ཆེས་བསྐུལ་མ་མཛད་པ་དང་། ཕྱིས་སུའང་དོན་གཉེར་ཅན་འགའ་ཡིས་བསྐུལ་བ་དང་། རང་ཉིད་ཀྱང་གཞུང་ཆེན་པོ་འདི་ལ་མོས་པའི་ཡིད་ཀྱིས། ཕྱིས་སུ་ཤིང་རྟ་ལོར་གདན་ས་ཆེན་པོ་ཀཿཐོག་ཏུ་མི་ཕམ་འཇམ་དབྱངས་རྣམ་པར་རྒྱལ་བས་མངོན་རྟོགས་རྒྱན་བཤད་པའི་ཞོར་ལ་བྲིས་ཏེ་ཞག་གསུམ་ལ་གྲུབ་པར་བགྱིས་པ་མངྒ་ལཾ།།

The Author's Colophon

The five texts of Maitreya are not specifically designated in the *Karchak Denkar*[65] and other catalogues of texts as belonging chronologically to the early translation period, but there is ample historical evidence that they were, in fact, translated then. Since that was a time when khenpos, acharyas and other learned masters abounded and Buddhism in India was still in its full flower, there is no dispute whatsoever as to the quality of the translations done then.

The supreme of Bodhisattvas, the Regent of the Victor,
with consummate insight,
Composed these texts, which flawlessly explain the intent of
the Victor's teaching
And clarify how the heirs of the Victor are to live. May they
spread delight!
May the flawless teaching of the Victor spread throughout the
ten directions.

The lake that nestles among the snows of original nonconceptual
wisdom
Is the wellspring of the treasures of Dharma, the teachings
of noble ones,
Helping you and all other sentient beings to lead a happy life.
Through living it well, may we finish the training and so enjoy
its full maturation.

During the Fire Ox Year, a highly revered tulku requested me to write a commentary on this present work. This request was later reiterated by a number of sincere practitioners. Prompted by that and my own devotion for this great work, I, Mipham Jamyang Namgyal, wrote this during the Wood Horse Year at the great seat of KaTog in connection with teaching *The Ornament of Direct Realization.* The composition was completed in three days.

May it bring happiness and well-being.

།ཆོས་དང་ཆོས་ཉིད་ཟབ་མོ་རྣམ་འབྱེད་པའི། །གཞུང་འགྲེལ་མི་ཕམ་འཇམ་དབྱངས་
གསུང་ཁྲིད་འཕགས། །ལྷུན་གྲུབ་སྙེང་དུ་སྤྲར་དུ་འདུ་བྱེད་པོ། །ལྷག་བསམ་མཚུངས་
མེད་ཚེ་དབང་སྒྲོལ་མ་སྟེ། །ཡིགས་བྲུས་འདིས་མཆོན་དུས་གསུམ་དགེ་ཚོགས་ཀྱིས།
།གང་དེ་མ་ཕམ་འབྲེལ་བཅས་ཐམས་ཅད་པ། །སྲས་བཅས་རྒྱལ་བའི་གདམས་པའི་
སྣོད་གྱུར་ཏེ། །ཆོས་ཀུན་མཉམ་པ་ཆེན་པོའི་དོན་རྟོགས་ཤོག། ||
།ཅེས་མདྣ་ལས་སྨོན་པ་དགེ།། ||

Dedication

This commentary on the text distinguishing the profound points of phenomena and pure being arose spontaneously. It was put into writing by the one with unparalleled motivation, Tsewang Drolma. May the merit accruing to this be equal to all the virtue of the three times and reach all sentient beings. May this connect them with the invincible Maitreya, transforming them into suitable vessels for the teachings of the victors and their heirs. May they realize the great equality of all phenomena.

May the power of virtue fulfill this aspiration prayer!

Bibliography

(Titles lacking Sanskrit and/or Tibetan equivalents are not found in those languages.)

Buddha Nature by Maitreya
Theg pa chen po'i rgyud bla ma
Mahayanottaratantrashastra (or Ratnagotravibhagamahayanottaratantra-shastra)

Distinguishing Phenomena and Pure Being by Maitreya
Chos dang chos nyid rnam par 'byed pa
Dharmadharmatavibhaga

Distinguishing the Middle from the Extremes by Maitreya
Dbus dang mtha' rnam par 'byed pa
Madhyantavibhaga

Jewel Ornament of Liberation by Je Gampopa
Dwags po thar rgyan (or Dam chos yid bzhin nor bu thar pa rin po che'i rgyan)

Miraculous Key by Khenpo Tsültrim Gyamtso Rinpoche
'Phrul gyi lde mig

Ten Great Prayers of a Bodhisattva
Byang chub sems dpa'i smon lam chen po bcu

The Buddha Within by Shenpen Hookham
Albany: SUNY Press, 1991

The Mosaic of the Rare and Supreme Ones, Requested by Kashyapa
Dkon mchog brtsegs pa'i 'od srung gis zhus pa'i mdo
Maharatnakuttisutra

The Ornament of Direct Realization by Maitreya
Mngon rtogs rgyan
Abhisamayalankara

The Ornament of the Sutra Collection by Maitreya
Mdo sde rgyan
Sutralankara

The Samadhi Wherein the Appearance of Heat is Attained
Drod snang ba thob pa'i ting nge 'dzin

The Sutra from the Journey to Srilanka
'Phags pa lang kar gshegs pa'i mdo
Lankavatarasutra

The Sutra Presenting Nonconceptual Retention
Rnam par mi rtog pa'i gzungs bstan pa'i mdo

The Sutra Requested by Maitreya
Byams pa zhus pa'i mdo
Maitripariprichchasutra

Notes

1 "Tushita," dga' idan, translates as "The Joyous Realm."

2 The two Ornaments are *The Ornament of Direct Realization* and *The Ornament of the Sutra Collection*. The two Distinctions are *Distinguishing Phenomena and Pure Being*, and *Distinguishing the Middle from the Extremes*.

3 According to the order in which they are listed here, the first of the five treatises would be *The Ornament of Direct Realization*; the last, *Buddha Nature*; and the middle three, *The Ornament of the Sutra Collection*, *Distinguishing the Middle from the Extremes*, and *Distinguishing Phenomena and Pure Being*.

4 "Prajnaparamita," shes rab pha rol tu phyin pa, is, in this context, a collective name applied to the teachings on emptiness as presented at the middle level, that is, the second turning of the Wheel of Dharma. Literally, the term "Prajnaparamita" translates as "transcendental knowledge."

5 "Sugatagarbha," bde gshegs snying po, "the heart essence of the one who has passed into bliss" is synonymous with buddha nature.

6 "Family," rigs, is sometimes also translated as "potential" in this context. For a description of the five families, i.e., the fivefold classification of the potential for achieving buddhahood, see Gampopa's *Jewel Ornament of Liberation*, chapter one.

7 "The three natures," rang bzhin gsum, also called "the three essentials" or "the three essential aspects of existence," are kun brtags (Skt., parakalpita), translated as "the completely imputed" or "imaginary nature;" gzhan dbang (paratantra), "the dependent nature;" and yongs grub (parinispanna), "the actually existent" or "perfectly present nature."

8 "The five prevailing themes," chos lnga, are: name, grounds, concept, original wisdom, and suchness.

9 The eightfold collection is a conventional division of consciousness in terms of the five sensory forms of consciousness, the rational (also called mental) consciousness, the afflicted mentality or klesha mind (which is the consciousness that conceives of "I" and "mine"), and the all-inclusive base consciousness. The term "sevenfold collection" refers to the first seven of these; "sixfold collection," to the first six.

10 "The Mother" is a collective name applied to teachings contained in the Prajnaparamita sutras.

11 See n. 7 with regard to the three natures.

12 Contrary to prevalent English usage, titles are frequently abbreviated in Tibetan. This custom has been adopted here due to the length of the full title. *Distinguishing Pure Being* is thus an abbreviation of *Distinguishing Phenomena and Pure Being.*

13 The Yogacharamadhyamaka corresponds in this context to the Shentong school.

14 "Learned teacher" is a translation of pandita. In this case, it refers to the Kashmiri Khenpo Mahadzana.

15 "Phenomenal world," chos can, is a synonym for "phenomena," chos. It is contrasted with "pure being," chos nyid, dharmata. Literally, "chos can" means "the bearer of pure being," referring to any phenomenon. "Chos nyid" can also be translated as "the quality itself," in which case "chos can" means "that which bears the quality."

16 The word "maitreya," byams pa, means "loving kindness."

17 "Actualized directly," mngon sum nyid du bya ba, could be translated as "experienced" or "met directly."

18 As defined in Tibetan medicine, the eye disorder referred to here (Tib. rab rib) is related to an imbalance of the phlegm. One of the effects accompanying this illness is the appearance of dark lines resembling filaments of hair in the visual field. This has been assumed here and throughout to correspond to gray cataracts.

19 In this present context, "symbolic expression," rnam par rig byed, customarily refers to language, defined broadly as rnam 'gyur—"expression through images"—meaning any set of visible or audible symbols conveying meaning. This would include letters, words and phrases, mathematical and musical symbols and so on, and also body language, where posture, hand and finger positions, and other physical signals vital to social ritual are taken to convey a certain meaning by members of a given group, viz., by those sharing such patterns.

20 gzhan lta ba la 'jug pa literally means "one enters into the views of others," or alternatively, "one engages in watching others." This has been translated broadly here due to Rinpoche's explanation, where he used the example of the behavior of chicks being based on watching and then copying adult birds' behavior.

21 "Image" is understood broadly here as "impression," referring to the five sensory impressions as well as the mental impression of these that presents itself to the rational consciousness.

22 This whole paragraph could also be translated, "What are being called 'outer objects observed in common' *are not referents existing as something extrinsic to or other than consciousness, precisely because they are* appearances comprising *common experiences* shared by a variety of beings whose mindstreams are not the same. But this is what proves that they are not something other than perceptions and these are the perceptions of mindstreams that differ."

23 "Mind" here refers to "primary conscious mind," gtso sems, which is another name for the sixfold collection of consciousness. "Mental states," sems byung, is also sometimes translated as "mental factors" or "mental events," of which there are fifty-one classified at the sutrayana level.

24 Lit., "arises in its image."

25 The word "exist" is not stated in Mipham Rinpoche's commentary but was supplied by Rinpoche in explaining this commentary.

26 For an explanation of the sixteen types of emptiness, see Maitreya's Madhyantavibhaga.

27 "The subject taught," brjod bya, and "its formulation," rjod byed, are also translated as "the signified factor" and "the signifiers," as in the definition of pure being and elsewhere.

28 The Tibetan word bsgom is normally translated as "meditation" but more literally means "habituation."

29 Rinpoche explains this passage as follows. The texts related to the shentong view distinguish between two types of suchness or nirvana: naturally pure nirvana and nirvana which has been purified of superficial stain. The former refers to the ultimate nature, i.e., the buddha nature, which is present from the very beginning and during all three phases of development, namely, during the base, path, and fruition stages, and whose essence is free of any stain or imperfection whatsoever. The latter refers to nirvana, seen from the perspective of its being the fruition of the path.

It is evident that this distinction is a matter of pure convention, since the nirvana achieved through the path is none other than the actualization of "that untouched by stain," i.e., that nature which has been present from the very outset. Thus, the essence of transformation consists, not in a change in the basic nature, but in a definitive elimination of everything that is "other" than, or not inherent to, that nature.

30 Dharmadhatu, chos kyi dbyings, translates as "expanse of qualities."

31 Dharmakaya, chos sku, translates as "body of qualities."

32 Sambhogakaya, longs spyod rdzogs pa'i sku, translates as "body of complete enjoyment."

33 Nirmanakaya, sprul pa'i sku, translates as "emanation body."

34 "Self-manifestation," rang snang, refers to non-dualistic experience. This term is contrasted with gzhan snang, referring to dualistic perception.

35 Shravakas, nyan thos, translates as "listeners;" Pratyekabuddhas, rang rgyal, as "solitary realizers."

36 This refers to a particular type of emanation body, namely, an historical buddha, also called "supreme nirmanakaya."

37 "Overestimation," sgro 'dogs, could also be translated as "doubt" in this context.

38 The word "gzhi" has been omitted, since it also means "ground." It is a word in the commentary whose only function is to indicate the sense of the word "gnas" in the root, since "gnas" can be interpreted in many ways. Once translated as "ground," another word, other than "support," is not needed to clarify the sense intended here.

39 "To remain in this natural state," rang bzhin du byed pa; KTGR explains here that byed pa is to be understood in the sense of gnas pa, which translates as "to remain."

40 The word "bskyed," translated as "develop," only applies in a conventional sense, since there is no increase or decrease in original wisdom, only a change in the obscurations covering it and the degree of realization of it.

41 The four types of logic are: the logic of general relations, ltos pa'i rigs pa; the logic of specific relations, bya ba byed pa'i rigs pa; the logic of valid cognition, tshad ma'i rigs pa; and the logic of nature, chos nyid kyi rigs pa.

42 This refers to the method practiced at the Shravaka level of conceiving of one's own and others' bodies as being composed of thirty-six repulsive substances as a means of overcoming desire in its coarse, naive form.

Rinpoche's commentary on this point is as follows: This is an example of a method belonging to the provisional type of teachings (drang don), meant to lead on to the next level, where the suchness or empty nature of the object of desire perceived and its perceiving mind are understood. Yet again, if one clings to the consciousness empty of the dualism of perceived and perceiver as truly existent, path again becomes obstacle and the definitive goal (nges don), naturally present wisdom (rang byung ye shes) which is empty both of dualism and of all conceptual elaborations, is not realized.

43 "As ends in themselves," yon tan; literally, "as excellent qualities."

44 The word brtag, translated as "observation," is the future form of rtog, "to conceptualize." As the word is used here, it refers to the absence of the actual process of a sensory consciousness perceiving its object. Normally, sensory consciousness is taught to be nonconceptual, but in this context its activity is conceptual in the sense that it involves the duality inherent in the subtle act of measurement constituting the process of perception. In other words, to perceive an object, the sensory consciousness must distinguish that object from everything that is not that object, and this is a subtly conceptual operation.

45 "Extreme" (mtha') is also translated as "speculation" or "theoretical conclusion," "limiting view," "limit," etc., indicating any conclusion arrived at through conceptual intellect (blo).

46 The six factors mentioned in this enumeration are identical to the six just named in each of the corresponding lists above, although the first is called "act of observation" above and "analysis" here. It refers to the activity of a sensory consciousness taking note of a sensory datum. It is here referred to as "analysis" for the same reason that an act of observation is said to be conceptual, as explained in note 44.

47 "Everything that goes with" any dualistic appearance for an ordinary confused intellect is, first, the assumption that perceived and perceiver both exist because they appear to do so, and, second, the process of formulation.

48 The point here is that there is no experience of the center of space, because, as the Buddha taught, space has no outer boundaries and, therefore, no center.

49 "Overestimation," sgro 'dogs, also translated as "exaggeration" or "superimposition," means "claiming existence for that which does not exist"; for example, thinking that the snake one is attacked by in a dream actually exists, which comes of not recognizing that one is dreaming. "Denial," skur 'debs, means "claiming non-existence for that which exists," i.e., denying any sort of existence of phenomena, which do "exist" as mere appearance. An example here would be denying the existence of the image of the snake in the dream.

50 "Fixation on theoretical conclusions," mthar 'dzin pa, could also have been translated as "clinging to extremes."

51 For a description of the four levels of meditative concentration and how examination (rtog) and analysis (dpyod) relate to them, see the chapter on karma in the *Jewel Ornament of Liberation.*

52 "Equilibrium of Cessation," 'gog snyoms, is the name of a formless samadhi belonging to the "peak of existence," the highest level of samsaric god realms. "Cessation" here does not refer to "cessation of suffering" but to a state so vague that one cannot speak of there being either clear notions or no notions at all.

53 "Entertaining attributes," mtshan 'dzin, can also be translated as "assigning labels."

54 The sense of "concrete" here involves a subtle extension of one of the term's definitions, namely, "characterized by or belonging to immediate experience of actual things or events," (cfr. *Merriam-Webster's Collegiate Dictionary*). Having eliminated pseudo nonconceptuality, the concrete characteristic, i.e., the actual nonconceptuality belonging to original wisdom, is what remains. It fits the definition of "concrete" by being what is actually there as opposed to being imagined. It also fulfills that definition by being the immediate object of experience, even though wisdom-awareness is the "observer," not a dualistic consciousness.

See Madhyantavibhaga, chapter 5, under the ten forms of freedom from error associated with vipashyana as defined in Mahayana for an equivalent use of the term "concrete characteristic" (rang mtshan).

55 "Distorting filter" is a translation of rab rib, which normally translates as "eye disorder" or "cataracts."

56 In the following section, Mipham Rinpoche elucidates the effects of nonconceptual wisdom in terms of what are called "the five forms of result." For the precise definitions of these, see Khenpo Tsültrim Gyamtso Rinpoche's *Miraculous Key.*

57 The term here translated as "the result attained by a gifted being," skyes bu byed pa'i 'bras bu, refers in this context to the result arrived at by a bodhisattva who has developed nonconceptual wisdom.

In general, the term has the sense of "man-made result," since it refers to the result created specifically by the intentional activity of an individual. Here it designates the result of the endeavors undertaken by the practitioner in following the path and thereby triumphing over afflicting factors.

58 This second of the five forms of result, bdag po'i 'bras bu, is sometimes translated as "environmental result" or "result related to the setting." For example, in the karma chapter of the *Jewel Ornament of Liberation,* it refers to the type of country or environment in which the performer of a specific type of karmic action will be reborn. It is here translated as "subjective result," intimating the given subject's relation to the setting, since to call it "environmental result" would seem to indicate an effect produced on the subject by an environment, whereas it refers to the opposite, namely, the sort of environment an individual creates through his or her way of understanding things and the actions based on that. Since a realized bodhisattva has an unmistaken understanding of all phenomena, the origin par excellence of harmonious surroundings, the setting experienced is one of untainted happiness, meaning a happiness which does not degenerate.

59 The relation between a given sensory consciousness, its faculty and its specific type of object is nontransferable in the sense that the eye cannot see sounds, the ear cannot hear forms, and so on. It should be noted that this limitation only pertains to ordinary beings.

60 "Mistaken conceptual process," yang dag min pa'i kun rtog, is a term of such central importance in this and other texts of Maitreya that it has been translated with the same term wherever it appears; although, in certain contexts such as here, it might be better rendered as "incorrect interpretation."

61 The three types of knowledge are the knowledge deriving from listening, from reflection, and from meditation.

62 "Abstract idea," don spyid, could also be translated as "general idea," "general picture," "generalization," and so on.

63 "Purified of this," i.e., of this entertaining of attributes, which also translates as "clinging to attributes" or "clinging to labels."

64 "The expanse without remainder of aggregates," phung po lhag ma med pa'i dbyings, is a synonym for nirvana stressing the total cessation of the aggregates constituting a samsaric individual. In the context of the Shravaka and Pratyekabuddha paths, this is held to indicate the end of rebirth entirely, whereas, in the Mahayana context, it is held to indicate the end of rebirth of tainted aggregates only, without that preventing rebirth in an emanation body. The discussion of the present point in the text deals precisely with the reason for this, namely, that liberation and enlightenment are a matter of the complete transformation of a mindstream, not its complete annihilation.

65 A list of Buddhist works drawn up in the time of Tri De Tsongtsen by a group of translators residing at the castle of Tongtang Denkar.